In Good Hands

THE KEEPING OF

A FAMILY FARM

In Good Hands

THE KEEPING OF

A FAMILY FARM

Charles Fish

❧

Farrar, Straus and Giroux

NEW YORK

Library of Congress Cataloging-in-Publication Data
Fish, Charles.
In good hands : the keeping of a family farm / Charles Fish. — 1st ed.
p.   cm.
1. Agriculture — Vermont — History.   2. Farm life — Vermont — History.
3. Family farms — Vermont — History.   I. Title.
S451.V5F57   1995   974.3'704 — dc20   94-45918   CIP

In memory of my grandmother

PAULINE LESTER WILLIAMS

1881–1962

Keeper of the Old Ways

Acknowledgments

☙☙

For their suggestions and encouragement, I wish to thank my wife, Eleanor, and my friends Rosemary O'Donoghue and Burton Porter (colleagues at Western New England College), Carl McInerney, Dorothy Riccardi, and Elizabeth Bobrick. With generous hearts and unclouded vision, they helped me to see what had to be done.

I am grateful to my uncle Sherwin Williams for information that supplemented and repaired my memory of farm life, for access to family documents, and for his unstinting hospitality and affection. He is the last of his generation on either side of my family and my most direct link to the vanishing world of which I write.

I am most fortunate to have as agent John L. Hochmann and as editor Jonathan Galassi, editor in chief of Farrar, Straus and Giroux. Their superb professional services have been graced by unfailing attention and courtesy.

Some information I owe to *Rutland Town: A Collection of Stories Spanning over 200 Years of Town History*, published in 1991 by the Historical Society of Rutland Town. I was also helped by Paul A. Carnahan, librarian of the Vermont Historical Society.

This book often reads as if I were a bachelor, looking back on an orphaned childhood. In fact, I have lived for thirty-four years with the same devoted wife, and I have two fine sons, a brother with a family of his own, and grateful memories of a mother and father who loved and cared for me. If this were an autobiography, which it is not, they would all play much larger parts. In fact, no man lingers in loving memory more enduringly than my father. But that's another story.

CHARLES FISH

Contents

❧

❧

In Good Hands

August 5, 1944

For this date, forty-eight years ago, my diary reads as follows:

Billy came down and let me ride his poney. We had some watermelon today. The men put up the hay machines.

Charles

True stories have no end, but a storyteller must find boundaries, or else from three small sentences in a diary he could be drawn to the beginning of the world. This is the story of six generations on a farm in Rutland, Vermont, and of a vagrant scion, myself, who tried to make a journey of his wanderings.

In 1944, when I was seven, my mother and father sent me to the farm for the summer. It was where my mother had grown up; it was like the farm of my father's people not twenty miles away. They believed that farms were good for boys, and, besides, my mother was not well. It was not a strange place, I had known it from infancy, and I felt as much at home there as in my village seventy miles to the north. Now, a half century later, I can bring the place to life through the curious passages of memory. I absorbed it through skin, nose, ear, eyes, and tongue, and it lies within to be recalled.

Three short sentences make a small window in time. Looking through it, what do I see of the world that day?

It was the end of haying. Over the weeks I had followed the men from house to field, and had seen the hay fall and dry to be raked and gathered, drawn to the barns, and hoisted to the lofts by hayfork. It was partly my work, for I had signaled the tractor to stop when the fork load had reached the track at the top of the loft. Now wagons, rakes, and hay-loader were put up for the season. The watermelon was a reward. It might have been cooling in the watering trough in the creamery. Uncle Sherwin or Uncle Milo would have brought it to the house, and Grandmother would have cut it. We would have sat on the back porch off the kitchen near the bridal wreath of Grandmother's garden, and I would have spit seeds on the ground.

Billy Thomas, a boy on the neighboring farm, had ridden down on his pony. The two farms were separate now, but they were once a single property before the artificial boundary had divided the rich, flat field. Sometimes his dog came down and fought with our farm dog, Muggsy, a woodchuck killer.

Later I learned that Grandmother's grandfather, Henry Whitlock Lester, bought the land in 1836 for $3,500, earning for himself, in my mind, the title of Founder. When he died in 1864, at age 58, he left half of his real estate, which included more than the farm, and $11,248.14 to William Henry Lester, my great-grandfather. My great-grandfather left it to several children, and one of them, my great-uncle Milo Lester, bought out the others and then, in turn, left it to my uncle Sherwin Lester Williams. This uncle, one of his sons, Larry, and his grandson, Paul, still live and work there.

Six generations of my blood have called it home. Though a

wayward shoot, I could not, if I wanted to, extricate myself from this piece of earth. I carry in memory pasture and meadow, corn and hay, chickens, pigs, cows, and horses, cedar, maple, elm, and oak, tractors, harrows, plows — all things touched by the old ones or touching them. Not even now, nearly a lifetime after my summer there and the keeping of my diary, nor after revolutions of thought and habit, have I entirely escaped the commands of the guardian spirits who inhabit the house and barns, the meadows and streams of this eighty-acre farm. But I am an apostate. I have not kept the faith. From peaks foreign to those whose issue I am, I have seen strange visions and have embodied the founder's fear that "collegiate courses" would spoil a man for any work "in the least beneficial or practical for use." I am a traveling man, but my journey is a journey in time, and the destination is myself.

In 1944 Grandmother was sixty-three, Uncle Milo sixty, Uncle Sherwin thirty-one, his wife, my Aunt Ellrena, thirty-two. I celebrated my eighth birthday that summer.

In my attempt to remember, question, and explore, I made use of five family documents: the founder, Henry Lester's, essay on God's plan, agriculture, politics, and morality; his essay on horses and horsemen; a letter to the founder from his father, Moses Lester; Grandmother Williams's reminiscences of family and farm; and my own boyhood diary. These affirmations of a way of life appear in whole or in part at the end of the book; excerpts from them appear at the beginning of each chapter. They bear witness to a tradition that this book both celebrates and interrogates.

When my fingers touch the brittle paper of these documents, when my eyes decipher the fading ink, I am stirred by something both intimate and remote. Nostalgia threatens, the old china and teacups of the spirit. Even as I submit to its spell, I distrust and fear it, for above all I want clarity, clarity about the nature of things, including my own being. I have learned that what most obscures clarity is not the veil of error or the dust of neglect or even the selective vision of a historical moment in time, obstructive as each may be. The most impenetrable obscurity lies within myself.

One summer I lived on a hilltop in Vermont and divided my time between reading and fishing. Each was a kind of searching and each imposed conditions. To catch rainbow trout in Little River or browns in the Lamoille, I had to know or guess what they ate and when. The quarry in my reading was more elusive, not only what was said and why, but my relation to it. With an immodesty never outgrown, I wanted to learn more about the nature of things, the generic, and about my own peculiarities. I was both fish and fisherman.

It was at such points of intense, troubled reflection that the farm diary reentered my imagination. Retrieved from the family's papers, it proved a passageway through which I could revisit the being I was, the conditions of my early childhood, and the changing character of the age. I found then and I find now that, although a narrow door, this brief, spare book opens into the abundant memories of a vanished time.

Fishing in Lake Champlain once, I brought up not a bass or a pike but a writhing eel. The waters of the past contain odd creatures too, and it may have been fear that led me to put the diary away. I wanted understanding, but there is always more at stake: pride, loyalty, affection, gratitude; comfort, habit, pleasure; duty, obligation, piety. Old certainties pale with time, and I had long swung between devotion and exploration, straying from the fold in the discovery of new powers and pursuits.

Now, years later, I return to the diary and the world it evokes. The diary belongs to two realms, to the daily round of activities in which tradition and the family virtues held sway, and to the journey into the self. Although it had at most barely crossed the boundary of this latter realm — it contains no anguished introspection — if Grandmother could have looked forward to the interior wanderings of which this slim record was the first step, she might have suggested a different intellectual exercise. If she could have seen her grandson's latent self-absorption as clearly as she saw her own duties and principles, she would have burned the book and sent him out to work.

I · The Farm

He next created man in his own image, male and female created he them, and gave them dominion over the earth, the sea, the fishes, the beasts, the birds, the herb-yielding seed, and the fruit-bearing tree.

HENRY LESTER, *Man Made for Agriculture*

And so Grandfather [the founder] and Grandmother Lester, having decided they would go to Rutland to live, left their home in the wilderness of Chittenden, where they lived ten miles from any neighbor on land that is now flooded by waters of the Chittenden dam. They bought this farm of a man named Hodges. It is located on the Pittsford road about three miles north of Rutland City, or Village, as it was then called. The village at that time comprised only a few buildings on North Main Street.

PAULINE WILLIAMS, *As I Remember*

I went down street and got a new pair of tennis shoes and two packages of bbs also two banana-splits. I am down on the farm for the summer. I got my bb-gun and bow and arrows.

Grandma and I went fishing. I caught three fish and pulled one out but fell off my hook back into the water and I lost him . . . We saw a kingfisher dive for a fish the first time in my life. finished potatoes today.

I went to Sunday school today. I took my lunch up on the big rock and ate it. I cut my knee on a nail, and spilled paper dye down my back. Joan fell through some rotten boards and landed on some sawdust.

CHARLES FISH, *Diary Book*

❧

North of the city of Rutland, on the east side of U.S. 7, the house still stands, large, two-story, white, with kitchen ell and attached barns. Built in the 1840s, it stood so close to the original house that when it was finished, the family passed some of the furniture from window to window. The old house was torn down, and the new one remained more or less unchanged until about 1900, when my great-grandfather William Lester added a wrap-around porch, replaced the small-paned windows with large panes, added the stamped-tin ceiling, and, to the regret of his descendants, removed the fireplace and Dutch oven.

Recalling the compact diversity of life sheltered by this succession of roofs, in memory I am a child again, it is the summer I turned eight, and I walk through the house. I enter the front door, used only for funerals, step into a hallway with the photographs of my ancestors, including the founder and his wife, pass into the parlor, which holds the piano, more photographs, the antique curly-maple secretary desk (made beyond memory by someone in the family), the tree at Christmas, and the casket when someone dies. Uncle Milo will lie here a few years later, and the family will gather to say goodbye. The parlor opens into the living room, where in the evening Grandmother reads the Bible and does her needlework. Next I enter the dining room with its oak table that holds us all at Thanksgiving, the maple butler's desk, the bay window with its squares of colored glass and Grandmother's plants — including the cactus nearly as old as she is — the dent in the tin ceiling where Uncle Sherwin as a boy bumped when tossed in a blanket, and the closet with its checkers, books, and the deceptive candy tin with a jack-in-the-box to jump at me when I open it. More than birthdays, more than Christmas, it was Thanksgiving in this room that imprinted on my heart an image of family felicity, uniting the generations in storytelling and laughter.

Several of the doors are extra wide. Years later, in Grandmother's reminiscences, I will read that the founder wanted them wide enough to admit big bags of wool to be stored in the attic. It took a carpenter all winter to make them. From the dining room I go to the kitchen with its oiled maple floor, the soapstone sink and old iron faucets which snap with electricity during thunderstorms, the cast-iron wood-burning cookstove, the woodbox big enough for Uncle Sherwin to nap on after midday dinner, and the rocker where Uncle Milo dozes in the evening. Off the kitchen is the bathroom with its soldered tin tub which grips the skin. From the kitchen I turn right (or south) into the storeroom full of baskets, boxes, and tools, then into two bays which house the car and the International pickup, and from there into the horse barn, which holds a workbench as well as horses and where Uncle Milo, if urged, will lift the great anvil with one hand, a hand measuring eleven inches from thumb to little finger.

Along the way, I have missed the bedroom where Grandmother, a widow, sleeps alone and where, on an old wooden chest, milk-paint red, she keeps a tray with tortoise-shell combs and long strings of beads, blue, green, and black; the room where her brother, my uncle Milo, a bachelor, sleeps alone; the pantry, whose old wooden cupboards hold the dishes, pots, and pans; and the unheated back pantry, cold storage in winter, on whose open shelves lie a hundred oddments.

I have missed, too, the second floor, home of Uncle Sherwin, Aunt Ellrena, and their two sons, Larry and Gareth, and the great attic with its pegged roof rafters and its chests of old papers, books, and clothes; and beneath it all the dirt-floored cellar, cool and dark, with the big round wood furnace, the potato bin, the jars of canned goods, and, under some boards, water faintly glimmering, the dug well which supplies the house.

Standing at the horse-barn door, I can see the house, the road, and, across the road, the cow barn, but at the end of the driveway, nearer and more commanding, is the giant elm, older than the family's possession of the land. Home at various times to golden orioles, red squirrels, and bees, a hitching post for breaking colts in the early days of the farm, and shade for tramps when the country was filled with wandering men, it is the farm's most conspicuous landmark and one of the largest elms in the state. At its death in 1983, a victim of the Dutch elm disease which will take all but two of the twenty-one elms on the farm, it will be two hundred years old, one hundred feet tall, and eight feet in diameter. At certain angles of the sun, it shades an acre of ground.

Turning east away from the tree and road, I go behind the horse barn to the attached pigpens where I have watched my uncle shoot rats with a .22 revolver. Farther into the field stand the old corn barn and another pigpen. Turning north, behind the house, I see the henhouse where I sometimes take eggs from reluctant hens that peck my hand. Along the north side of the house, heading back toward the road, I pass, at the edge of the field, Grandmother's flower garden, a surprising burst of splendor in a setting of severe practicality.

When Grandmother was a child, the only vehicles on the road were horse-drawn. The road was friendly then; it invited visitors and made it possible to go to town. It had attracted the founder and his wife in 1836 when, as Grandmother said, they "left their home in the wilderness of Chittenden, where they lived ten miles from any neighbor." The town was a small village then, but as it grew into a city, the country road grew into a state highway, and in 1931, five years before I was born, it was paved. By 1944 it is still the vital link to the world beyond, but it is no longer friendly. Dogs and cats are killed there, and old men and children are in constant danger. Northbound cars find themselves at the beginning of a straightaway, and southbound are at maximum speed. The tale is still told of the motorcycle that smashed against the elm, killing the rider. The time will come when Uncle Sherwin can count three hundred cars every twenty minutes.

I cross the road. Facing me is the big red barn which William Lester, my great-grandfather, son of the founder, built in 1882, marking the date and his initials on the door in nails still to be seen. The door slides to the right to allow hay trucks and wagons to enter. Sawdust bins and calf pens line one wall; along the other and above are the great storage mows for hay. Overhead I have tested my courage and balance by walking the open beams spanning the loft. I am too young for lovers, but in years to come, recalling stories of country sweethearts and stirred by desire, I will lie dreaming on the sweet, rustling, resilient mounds of hay, isolated from the world and free to imagine pleasures of intolerable intensity. In this summer of my childhood, when my friend, a neighbor's daughter, fell through the rotten boards in the loft to the floor below, scratching her legs, I did not know what moved me, but long after my memory of alarm fades, I will still see the dress above her waist and the bright red streaks on the white of her thighs.

There is other blood, too. Removing a floorboard reveals an iron strap under which, at butchering, Uncle Sherwin tied a cow's halter rope, pulling her nose to the floor. I heard the thwock of the maul on the head. I saw the animal slump to her knees. The throat opened to the jab and slice of the double-edged sticking knife, and the torrent of the brightest red I ever saw poured through the floor for the rats. Minutes later the cow was hanging from a yoke through her hamstrings, the head severed. Soon she was disemboweled and skinned. The windlass that raised her was rigged by my great-grandfather.

At a corner of the main barn I come to the silo, where I draw a breath of corn ensilage vapor, moist, hot, and sweetly rank. In newer, tighter silos, poison gas accumulates and farmers have been found dead in them. I enter the stable, an ell off the south side of the big barn. To the right, mounted on the wall, is the vacuum pump that runs the Empire milking machines. After the great flood of 1947, the farm will switch to a Surge, and Uncle Sherwin will say that if he had but one cow and she had but one tit, he would still use a Surge. The vacuum pump goes tookh, tookh, tookh, soothingly. Everything is rhythmic and measured here, the breathing of the cows tied in their stanchions, their lazy chewing, the slurping of their muzzles in the water bowls, the milking-machine cups pulling at the heavy bags, the calf sucking my fingers as I teach it to drink from a pail, the bumping of the wooden wheels of the old ensilage cart as it comes down the incline to the alley in front of the cows, even the process of digestion with its periodic discharge of urine and manure. My job is to walk along with a hoe, scraping the splatters into the gutter and pulling sawdust back to absorb the moisture.

Digestion can break the pattern—an ill-timed cough will propel manure like a bullet against the wall or a passerby. And the bull, placid now in his pen of heavy oak, is capable of unpredictable rage, never to be trusted, always to be led by a staff and the ring in his nose.

I have seen the act. Much later I will recall the bull's power and urgency when a cow in season is brought to him, the snorting and blowing, and the astonishing ease and lightness with which he rises to mount her. His penis is thin but very long, and it begins to discharge before entering. In a moment it is over and the bull is back on four feet. A dead bull isn't good for much, but his penis, dried, makes a fine whip.

I walk the length of the stable behind the cows to the creamery where the forty-quart milk cans wait in the cooler for Uncle Sherwin to take them to the dairy. Years before, the cans cooled in the watering trough where on certain days in the summer, and always on the Fourth of July, a watermelon would float. The far side of the trough is open to the barnyard, where the cows pass to and from the stable. The room smells faintly of milk and strongly of the iodine cleanser used on pails and cans, a clean smell. Farmers are not yet required to store their milk in bulk tanks, expensive machines the need for which will destroy many small farms in Vermont.

The creamery door opens to the barnyard, part of which is enclosed by the two barns and a fence. Here the cows gather to enter the stable, and the ground is sticky with manure. Here the bull is let out to exercise and get some air. Across the barnyard to the south of the stable is the machinery shed, and beyond is the lane leading to the path under the bridge where the cows cross to the east side of the road.

The bridge is open, modern, concrete; but not many years before, it was covered and wooden, known as the Lester bridge, and was just one of four over this river, East Creek, all built by one man between 1849 and 1876 and now all gone, destroyed by flood or replaced by modern structures. This is a valley farm, and the river, which bounds the farm at the south, occasionally leaps its banks; in 1947 it will dump sand and uprooted trees on the farm, nearly killing Uncle Sherwin and Clarence, the hired man.

I come to the hole beneath the bridge where one day, as Grandmother watched, I found myself suddenly and wonderfully swimming, dog-paddling my way from one side to the other. Upstream there is a deeper, broader pool the farm calls the old swimming hole, with a strip of sand on one side, on the other a flat black rock, hot in the sun, and, in between, a stretch of smooth water covering, as a veil, uncertain recesses and indeterminate shadows. I have caught fish in the river, dace and red-finned salmon, the latter an elusive species unknown to my adulthood. There are trout, too, but they are for the skill of later years. I have seen the blue flash of a kingfisher as it snatched a fish from the water, and I have seen mink play along the bank in rapid undulations.

Walking east along the edge of pasture and stream, I come to the big rock meadow where an abrupt outcropping provides a place to climb and picnic. Even to my mind as a boy, the rock suggests permanence or, as I will later think, an anchor binding the shifting surface of the farm to the earth's core. The smooth face of the west side reveals the hand of man, for here were blasted off foundation stones for the house. I turn to the north along a smaller brook, which marks the east boundary of the farm. I come to a hill, the sugar bush (a stand of sugar maples). Each spring Uncle Sherwin and Uncle Milo make syrup in an ancient wooden sugarhouse at the edge of the woods, collecting the sap in a large tank drawn on a sled by two horses, the last team but one in this era of tractors and trucks.

Grandmother and my great-uncles were alive at the very turning point of modern mechanization, born before roads knew a single automobile or farms a truck. I was born into the thinnest shadows of the vanishing era, and it is not an old horse that connects me with my youth but an old tractor, a John Deere, which will be new on the farm when I work there in high school, rebuilt thirty-six years later, and still in use.

From the back of the sugar woods, I can see, in the valley to the east, the farm my father wanted to buy and where I might have spent my childhood; a dispute over a meadow killed the sale. Descending the sugar-woods hill along the north boundary, I come to the hemlock spring, with its enameled ladle and never-failing flow of water at the roots of an old tree. Grandmother recalled that the spring supplied a sheep barn in the early years, and Uncle Milo used to keep fat trout there until the neighbor's tenant farmers discovered them. The spring is neither wide nor deep, but in my mind it leads down by inaccessible passages to some dark realm.

I cannot describe it, but even as a child there are for me points of concentration, intense foci where, as in the gathering of the sun's power by a magnifying glass, family talk has distilled the various essences of the life of the farm. The spring is one. The big rock is another, as are the swimming hole, the hayloft, the stables, the kitchen, the cedar swamp, and the meadow brook. Years later I will wonder if it was out of such intimacy, protected and prolonged beyond modern imagining, that the lesser gods of antiquity were born, tutelary deities, peculiar to their places.

I cross the flat along the north line, a barbed-wire fence dividing a field. Unlike a stream or tree line, this boundary appears to be perfectly arbitrary. The land on one side is indistinguishable from that on the other, and I see no reason why Uncle Milo should not own it all. I will later learn that the founder did own it all, but divided it between his two sons, and from one of them the north half passed out of the family. It is very clear in my mind that it does belong to someone else, and I already see, if dimly, that the farm's sense of itself requires a keen and formal recognition of boundaries, as if it cannot define what it is without knowing what it is not.

Continuing west across the road and another field, I come to the edge of the cedar swamp which lies on the neighbor's land to the north. I have ventured into it, but not often or far. It is dark and alien, unlike any other terrain in the valley, and I have no sense of its other extremities. In my imagination it could go on forever, and its very inaccessibility constitutes for me its enduring power.

Skirting the swamp, I come to the meadow brook which flows out of it, so small I can jump it and so gentle that its pools and undercut banks survive from year to year, sheltering brook trout in a contained world of illusory permanence. I gaze into it. I will come to know wilder waters, but in no contemplation of river or sea will I ever so completely lose myself.

The west boundary lies beyond the brook where the meadow yields to the slope of a rocky, juniper-strewn pasture. The pasture has a distinctive quality because it belongs to a farm — 150 acres, mostly hillside — of another great-uncle, Henry Lester. It seems that whatever makes Uncle Milo's farm the farm, its spirit I might later say, flows in diminishing waves up the hillside, whereas against other adjoining property it stops abruptly as against a dike.

It is the far side of the valley. I can look back east across the meadow, past the barn and the house and the field beyond, to the big rock meadow and the sugar bush, and farther still to blue hills and mountains. I see Pico, the mountain which, with Killington and Shrewsbury, dominates the range that divides the state, east from west. Generations ago the founder's eyes saw the varied topography as evidence of God's wise design, necessary for water to flow and gather and for the land to produce a variety of plants and trees. Up there somewhere is the farm's summer pasture, 125 acres of open and wooded hillside, nine miles away by dirt road from the back or east side of the farm. Each spring the young stock are herded up there; each fall they are herded back. I have walked it with them.

I head south now to the river across which is the fifty-acre farm that once belonged to the third great-uncle, Walter Lester, known as Uncle Bub; it is out of the family now and means little to me. I know that as the river leaves the farm it turns and flows south into the city, but it is vaguely disturbing that it should do so. It is not a city stream. It belongs to the farm. That it flows from the mountains down to the farm is less anomalous, perhaps because in flood it brings some of the wildness of woods and mountains to the cultivated valley floor.

The farm is nothing if not an artful form, the farmer, as the founder said, having "conquered by indomitable energy and perseverance the savage beasts, the savage men, the savage wilderness, and the more than savage clime." But more obviously than in man's other arts the matter is the natural world, ever ready to reestablish its primitive condition. As a child, I do not have words for it, but I am at home where the natural and the human meet: a meadow stopping at a stream, a barn standing in a field, a stone wall disappearing into woods. The built and cultivated things give me safety, comfort, pleasure (I am spared the constant struggle of my uncles' work), but it is the more obviously natural things that stir and excite me, not the least those that can be hunted and killed.

A short trek east along the river brings me back to the highway and the concrete bridge. I walk under the bridge and along the edge of the pasture toward the house, having circumambulated this bounded, cultivated patch of earth, legal and physical testimony to the faith of the founder and those before and after him who believed that "the supreme being made the earth for the use of man." Cars go by on the road. They pass through the farm, but they are not of it. In them are people who do not belong here.

II · The Grandmother

Out of the long ago I can see my grandmother Lester [the founder's widow] contentedly knitting in the little old Windsor rocking chair. As one watched her, you could plainly see pictured in her face the memories she cherished, her honor and integrity, her self-respect and conscience. In all these things she was a rich woman.

And even today, I hear very clearly out of the past Grandma's wise admonition "Waste not, want not." I can say with all truthfulness that I have tried to live up to this wise saying. If perchance I should have to go over the hill to the poorhouse, it will be with a clear conscience.

PAULINE WILLIAMS, *As I Remember*

I went down swimming with Grandma today.

I helped Grandma and aunt Ellrena pick peas but I ate more than I picked. I shucked them for Grandma.

The man who was captured yesterday was a homicidal maniac. they found him north east of Rutland city. I ran out of ammunition for my bb gun. grandma and I had dreams about him.

Childrens day at Chapel today. I recited my piece. It was a good program.

CHARLES FISH, *Diary Book*

⚜

Rereading my diary, I find Grandmother nearly everywhere, although she is seldom mentioned. She took me to Sunday school, she took me fishing and swimming, she told me the names of plants and birds and animals, she cleaned me when my bowels betrayed me, she cooked my meals, she let me sleep in her bed, she read to me, and she ran the household. She could drown kittens and bury dead babies, and if ancient customs had prevailed, if there had been a family altar, her knife could have drawn the sacrificial blood. But she was kind to the afflicted. Uncle Sherwin remembers that the tramps or knights of the road could expect a glass of milk and a sandwich; they were attracted, it was said, by a secret mark on the great elm, signifying the generosity of the house.

Every week she took me to the chapel for Sunday school and, for two weeks, sent me to Daily Vacation Bible School. The chapel was not church as I knew it in town. It was a Protestant chapel, short on doctrine and ritual, long on biblical stories, devotion, morality, and good works. Built in 1896 entirely by local effort at a cost of $1,075 and in continuous use ever since, it was a community chapel without denominational affiliation or professional clergy. Sunday school for children and adults was its chief activity, and all those who attended and ran it lived within five miles of the building. Some of its members also belonged to the regular churches in the city, but they reserved their participation there for high and solemn occasions, if at all. Weddings and funerals were often held at home.

The chapel was also a community center. Uncle Sherwin and Aunt Ellrena belonged to a theater group that put on plays in the building. Some forty-five years after my first summer on the farm, family and friends gathered there to celebrate my aunt and uncle's fiftieth wedding anniversary. Members now meet for monthly suppers "in the belief," as one account puts it, "that the world is a little better if you can sit down with your neighbors once a month to share a homemade pie." One hundred fifty years ago, the founder said, "Man was made a social being," and he probably meant by it both the political association, of which he saw the farmer as the chief maker and supporter, and the gatherings of families, which satisfied the desire for companionship.

"Today I went to church and got My Bible," I wrote. The next week I was given a piece to learn for Children's Day, and the third week I recited the piece and ventured a critical comment on the proceedings: "It was a good program." Later, in Bible School, I rose rapidly through the ranks: "I started as private and turned from private to corporal and from corporal to sergeant." And at the end of the session: "Daily vacation Bille school ended today. For learning Bible verses they gave prizes. I received a prize, it was a black walnut letter opener." By such appeals to the love of gain, glory, and ambition are the young brought to love virtue. Or so it was hoped.

Grandmother read her Bible every day. Abraham and Isaac were as familiar to her as the next-door neighbors. No historical consciousness, no higher criticism clouded her vision of the immediacy and relevance of the biblical record. For to her it was a record, an account of what was; it was not myth, legend, symbol, or folktale. Arguments over literalness or narrative inconsistencies did not bother her, and she did not engage in them. She would have said that she had enough to do understanding and following what was clear without troubling herself over what was not. Man's fate did not depend on logical coherence or scientific exactitude or the apprehension of theological niceties. His origin and destiny were clear, as were the moral requirements of the here and now. There was no gap for her between daily life on a Vermont farm in the mid-twentieth century and the life of the Jews or the early Christians two thousand years ago. It was not something she spoke of in so many words, but looking back I know that she carried in her mind a simple chronology in which the events of the Bible flowed through the centuries into her own lifetime without significant interruption. She shared with her grandfather, the founder, the belief that the "great architect of the universe" had so arranged things as to give her and her people a place and a purpose.

She did not send me to Sunday school, she went with me, and when she did so she was thinking not only of the boy I was but of the man she wanted me to become. It was partly family pride, no doubt, and partly the affection born of proximity, and partly some inexplicable compatibility (the diary records that we both dreamed about the escaped "homicidal maniac") that held us close even as my path diverged from hers, but it was also a clear notion of the requirements of manhood. That a boy should be free to choose opinions and principles like a shopper at a flea market would have struck her as preposterous. It would have appalled her that a family could be so lacking in self-confidence or casual about the roots of its being that it could leave so fundamental a matter to the vagaries of chance or the corruptibility of human nature. The founder wrote, ". . . let the farmer be proud that he belongs to that honorable, useful, healthful, rural, independent profession. Let him inculcate this sentiment into his sons and daughters. Let him educate in this faith and for this purpose."

And so she paid attention. She seldom preached, but by reminder and example she taught the importance of honesty, duty, charity, compassion, sexual restraint, clean speech, frugality, faith, love of country, and hard work. She was not theoretical, she did not categorize, she did not puzzle over the unity or separability of the virtues. She thought she knew what made a human being good and she wanted it for those she loved, just as she cherished the memory of it in her grandmother, the founder's wife, whose honor, integrity, self-respect, and conscience made her a "rich woman." Years later when my college letters began to show traces of my liberated vocabulary — mild expletives to display my wit and manliness — she checked me with the observation that she had noticed a certain change in my language which she thought unnecessary. She knew honest work could be intellectual or white-collar, a preacher's or doctor's, say, but inheriting her grandfather's partiality to manual labor, she liked calluses on a man's hands, and from time to time over the years she would feel my palms and make a joke about the state of my character.

On the sixth day of the visit, "Grandma and I went fishing. I caught three fish and pulled one out but fell off my hook back into the water and I lost him. We followed the river up to the end of Uncle Milos propperity. We saw a kingfisher dive for a fish the first time in my life. finished potatoes today."

I couldn't go to the river alone. On the days I fished or swam without other boys, she went with me. Fishing or swimming with her was fishing or swimming, not an expedition with her on which I fished or swam. It had nothing discernible to do with her wishes, plans, or expectations, and she did not exhort or cajole. She never fussed. She walked with a calm, even pace while I scampered; she sat quietly while I paddled about or dropped the worm in the water. She knew the names of the plants and animals, and through her I sensed without being told when something rare or beautiful revealed itself to us — the kingfisher's blue flash, the mink's brown, supple flow.

On first acquaintance her bearing must have invited respect rather than affection. About five feet three inches tall, of medium frame, with regular features, a firm mouth, and dark-gray hair wrapped tightly in a bun, she stood erect and looked at the world through rimless glasses with the steady gaze of an old photograph. Her hands were still. She made no apparent effort to observe, but nothing escaped her notice. She had the peculiar repose of one to whom the thought of impressing would never occur and who was herself not easily moved. She did not need to speak of dignity or self-confidence or self-esteem. She was who she was; she was there.

She was not, then, the kind of grandmother against whom I could work out whatever fevers of the soul might possess me. She never punished me, and with all her potential for severity she was never harsh. When in great shame I could not reach the bathroom in my desperate walk across the long flat from the neighbors, she neither smiled, scolded, nor frowned, but with the greatest composure stripped and bathed me. Three times a day she cooked for me and the household the solid farm diet of cereal, meat, potatoes, vegetables, and pie, and now and then the fish I caught. Some of the time at least — memory fails — I slept in her bed, and once when I had discovered the pleasant sensation induced by wriggling gently on my belly, she quietly asked me to stop, and I did. In the evening she often read to me, sitting on the living-room couch or in her kitchen rocker — the book, the smell of her hair, the touch of her gnarled arthritic hands, the feel of the stiff fabric of her dress, the clear articulation of her voice, the little smiles of delight and feigned surprise as the story unfolded, all blending for me in a circle of contentment. As I think of it now, I wonder what pattern of fulfillment was laid down there, what expectation of femininity, to challenge and complicate my manhood.

I remember her most vividly in the house, not only running it but presiding over it. I can still see her as she was, in her plain straight dress and apron, standing at the sink or stove, straining the house milk warm from the barn, setting the kitchen table where we ate all our meals except on special occasions, sweeping crumbs off the table into a miniature dustpan with a small, soft brush, watering her plants which filled the big dining-room window, sweeping the floor, or dusting the furniture. The house was clean, neat, and orderly, and was kept so by small, regular chores, not by erratic bursts of energy. She reminded others to do their small part, levying a ten-cent fine if someone forgot to carry his dishes from the table to the sink. If the chores were burdensome, I would not have guessed it as I watched Grandmother do them day by day.

These things a good maid might have done as well, however. What gave them their special quality was the quiet authority with which Grandmother handled everything that came her way. No mere laborer in this domestic garden, she cultivated souls with pots, pans, needle, and broom. When her husband died of tuberculosis thirty years before, leaving her with a two-year-old son and a seven-year-old daughter, she came back to the farm where she was born to keep house for her father, her children, and her bachelor brother (my uncle Milo), and over the years imposed her will on the household. Although like her brother she lent money at interest to people in the town, her true domain was the family and her deepest economic instincts were those of frugal conservation, not investment and expansion. No longer a wife, she was still the mother, the housekeeper, the arbiter of manners and morals, the interpreter of customs, the oracle of the temple. Her rule was gentle but far-reaching, and like all good monarchs she knew that a thread of necessity connects the lowest elements with the highest: woe to the king who ignores the flow of money, the games children play, or the way mothers and fathers amuse themselves. Crumbs were to be disposed of promptly, and I sensed, but could not have explained, a link between the efficient sweep of that little brush and the cosmic order represented by the weekly excursion to Sunday school.

Dirty boots were cleaned on the iron scraper by the back door or removed. Shirts were worn at table on even the hottest days of August. Except for the toast the men ate when they got up at four o'clock for morning chores, all meals were taken in common and were always served at the same time unless the urgency of field work postponed them. Food passed with a please and a thank you. The talk ranged from weather, crops, and cows to whatever appeared in the newspaper, but there was no swearing, not even the mildest four-letter words, and never an off-color story. As much as possible the roughness of farm life — the dirt and odors, the physical force and blood, the daily contention with imperfect machines and recalcitrant nature — was excluded from the house.

Looking back, however, I see that order was not maintained by mere exclusion. Grandmother was not a guard, the household was not a private retreat to be protected. No doubt she would have agreed with the founder that of all occupations agriculture "tends more than any other to lead the mind to religion, morality, and virtue," but her practice was more subtle and profound than his words. And so the household was to the entire farm as the heart to the body, sending the blood of moral purpose and correct action to all the parts and receiving in turn physical and economic means of support. One law or principle animated the whole and found in the household its clearest expression and in Grandmother its most devoted servant. She lived as if she believed that taste, manners, customs, and morals were deeply intertwined. She had read enough and seen enough of men and women to know that a man may smile and be a villain or that a rough manner may conceal a heart of gold; she knew man was an imperfect creature and that, no matter the effort, results were not guaranteed. But despite weaknesses and exceptions, which she recognized without fretting, she held to a unitary view of man and believed, in the most untheoretical and immediate way, that to expose one part to infection was to jeopardize the whole. If fortune had made her the founder of a kingdom and had allowed her political opinions to follow her deepest instincts about human nature, she would have chosen the children's books and games, and established the holidays and form of worship.

I think about the house, solid, big, heavily built with post and beam, substantial and dignified without ornamentation. A generation after it was built, the family added the large wrap-around porch and other niceties, hinting at a modest leisure the founder had not allowed himself. But even at the very beginning, this farm, unlike so many, did not pay for the handsome barn with a squalid house. A house is shelter. Whether it incarnates a household depends on the luck and wisdom of the family. The spirit of this household resided in the house and manifested itself in walls and woodwork, in windows and doors, in plants and pictures, and in tone of voice, turn of phrase, and nuance of gesture. What I felt as a child I now understand, that if Grandmother were more bookish she would have said that all aspects of the farm were necessary and honorable, integral to a way of life of which the finest expression was the household, which harmonized the claims of soul and body. What she did say was that it was all honest work, but she understood by that a more comprehensive order than mere compliance with the law. Shoveling manure or castrating pigs only made sense — or made its finest

sense — in the light of the manners, customs, and beliefs that it
supported. The continuance of the household was made possible
by manure and blood, but manure and blood made sense only in
the light of the household. And they could not by themselves have
called the household into existence. Its true origin was not economic, was not even coexistent with the building of house and
barns, although its physical birth, so to speak, its appearance as
a tangible expression, was an economic event.

All this was implicit in the domestic order, which reflected
a personal order, spiritual and physical. Apart from occasional
colds, Grandmother was not, in my memory, ever sick until she
contracted the heart disease which finally claimed her at eighty-
one. Her arthritis was a thing of the past, having left her with
hard, enlarged knuckles; she would challenge me to a duel, rap-
ping fists, and laugh when she made me quit. Not until I was a
man and learned more about the intricacies of family history did
I begin to suspect that her composure was not a gift of nature,
that her ordered ways may have been forged in higher heat than
her habitual calmness might suggest, and that her integrity and
rectitude came with a price. I have now come to think, to spec-
ulate, that even her good health was a victory over a rebellious
body which, but for her indomitable will, would have killed her
before I was born, for I know that the loose-topped dresses and
the handkerchiefs stuffed in the bosom concealed a double mas-
tectomy and that a severe heart attack had confined her to bed
for weeks. I wonder if cancer and heart disease were for her the
analogue to a long spiritual ordeal, the culmination and crisis of
an insurrection in her soul that she did not glory in or announce
or, perhaps, even understand. Once past it, the battle won or the
demands otherwise accommodated, she carried on with her life,
clearer than ever about her place, her duty, her spiritual destiny,
the only threat to her serenity the occasional outbursts of her

daughter whose own struggles had interlocked with hers. Outwardly, I imagine, her life changed little, if at all. There were no family stories of radical departures, no hints of eccentricity or difficult behavior. In the last thirty years of her life, the deepest forces of her nature, cultivated and shaped, achieved as great a harmony, if not on the grandest theme, as it is given to man to know. But there was a price. Harmonies not only include and express, they exclude and restrain.

They do so because the experiences of which character is built form a web, and every pattern is finite. Grandmother was a moralist, in some respects a rigid one, but she understood by character something more than adherence to a set of prescriptions and prohibitions. Although she would not have used the words, she understood character to be something like the bent of the soul, its cultivated inclinations. And she would have taken for granted what I had to discover, that the character and political fortune of a people are intimately connected.

But there is more to her story. The thread leads through the eye of a needle, to a garden, and into the labyrinth of the heart.

Despite her economy of spirit and motion, her fine adjustment of effort to the demands of the task, Grandmother put in a strenuous day. She never worked in the fields or barn as some farm women did, but she cooked, cleaned, washed, canned, mended, and no doubt managed other activities I can no longer remember. And she felt it, she got tired. She said, however, that when evening came and she took up her fancy work, her fatigue vanished. She was ready for the most precise and painstaking pursuit of beauty, although she would not have called it that. Her needlework, though conventional, was unusual in its range, intricacy, and harmony of design and color. She did not call herself an artist, or even a craftsman; she belonged to no associations, exhibited in no shows, and all that she made stayed in the house or went as gifts to children and grandchildren. Through a lifetime of quilts and afghans and lace, of stitching, crocheting, and knitting, some desire of her nature, something potentially magnificent, found its severely disciplined and circumscribed expression.

Perhaps the fancy work alone would not have engendered this speculation, but there was also the garden. Grandmother — this woman of bun-knotted hair, unpainted lips, plain dresses and shoes — built and tended a flower garden so opulent, varied, and rich that even I, for whom flowers were at most a passing interest, felt it as a voluptuous retreat, a splendid counterpoint to the functional sturdiness of the barns and the sensible comforts of the house. Bigger and more formal in design than most country gardens, it claimed its space from the field beyond as if to assert the needs of a part of the soul which corn and hay could not satisfy. Here was perfect order combined with sensuous delight, a clear design without severity, fecundity without confusion. Although I have fewer memories of the garden than of many other parts of the farm, they exist in a class of their own. Like certain dreams they juxtapose vivid details — a scent, the droop of a blossom, a moment's pause on a path — with a blur of visual impressions and currents of strong but indefinite feelings, erotic, no doubt, but an eroticism of the most diffuse and melting kind. Much of memory is sensuous and I can recall the smells of cows, horses, and woodchuck skins, of hair, dresses, coats, and overalls, and most of them are pleasant; but when a stray flower scent — sometimes the faint, musty sweetness of bridal wreath — evokes the garden, I am transported to a place of pure pleasure, of the keenest perception enveloped by the most delicious languor. None of the other pleasures of the farm, none of those available to me at least, was quite like it. Fishing and swimming were pleasures, but they were also activities and could be justified as useful, and killing woodchucks the same. Gardening was an activity, hard work in fact, but its end was only delight. The question, I remind myself, is the harmony of Grandmother's life and what possibilities it excluded or restrained. The garden was the work of her eye and her strong, gnarled hands in collaboration with the exuberant forces of nature: she planned and planted, clipped and weeded. Without her work there would be no garden. But perhaps the clipping and weeding were essential for other reasons as well. Perhaps she needed to earn her pleasure because of a moral economy which dictated that what is best is what we work for, or because the detached act of seeing and enjoying seemed to bring pleasure unmediated to the soul. Whatever the case, I imagine, the garden was an outpost of the spirit. When she paused from clipping and weeding and opened herself to the flood of color and scent, she had gone in that direction as far as she could go.

Grandmother was a second mother to me. She was the very center of family life, the figure in whom the pattern of virtue was most patently manifest. Only in the reflections of later years can I imagine what other currents may have welled up in her being, to be diverted from their most natural expression to the ends of family affection and the love of beauty. The essence of femininity for me, as I knew it from childhood, included the erotic only in a deeply transformed way. As a result, women in their fullness of being will always be for me mysterious and intriguing, not the growth or extension of something I have always known, but unfamiliar, desirable, obscure. I suspect that a woman constituted as Grandmother was can most readily and securely assume the guardianship of the household, that the transformation and generalization of the erotic may be characteristic of such high service. And I wonder if there can be high service without sacrifice.

My mother, Grandmother's daughter, endured great suffering, the roots of which were probably too deeply buried for her to trace even if she had subscribed to the analytic mode, which she did not, and which were certainly beyond my ken. Sometimes in a mood of sober reflection, other times in the pain of feelings she could neither understand nor accept, she dropped hints about her childhood that complicated my perspective and made me think that being a grandson is very different from being a daughter. There were incidents, common enough at any time, no doubt, and tame in comparison with the more lurid revelations of today, which in the context of the moral life of the farm and its little community loomed large and threatening. What appeared to me as principled firmness looked to my mother like myopic severity, an inability to handle with ease and reassurance the emotional struggles of a young girl.

Grandmother never spoke to me of her life with her husband, but I gathered that marriage was an interlude in a life that found its center elsewhere. A keeper of family records, she left in her papers no traces of her husband's ancestors or his several brothers whom I never met, although some of them lived nearby and survived Grandmother by many years. They were mentioned in the family from time to time, but they were less real than the neighbors. I eventually learned that my grandfather, Alden Williams, was the first rural mail carrier in the town, that he started November 1, 1899, and delivered to 600 people along a twenty-mile route, that he was one of a large family, that he was married for a few years, fathered two children, and died of tuberculosis. And that is all. When I drive by the house where my mother spent her earliest years, an old farmhouse on a hill overlooking the valley of the farm, these bare facts come to mind.

If there was a shadow over this side of life, there was also, I know, a disproportion between Grandmother's hardness and the sensitivities of my mother. Some of my mother's early photographs suggest a delicate loveliness, remote from conventional images of sturdy rural character. It was with a kind of fear that she told me how Grandmother would drown unwanted kittens and how, with unsentimental dispatch, she supervised the burial of a stillborn child in the family.

Grandmother, for her part, was nearly silent about the conflict with her daughter, but on one occasion, when I was perhaps fifteen, she came to me with tears in her eyes and said that I could not imagine the things my mother had said to her. I did not ask what they were and she did not say.

Uncle Sherwin, my mother's brother, was as hearty and robust as my mother was uncertain and tormented, inheriting Grandmother's toughness along with her capacity for loyalty and affection, illustrating how fortuitous is the association of nature and culture. In some kingdom of the imagination, there would be the wisdom and means to give each soul what it most deeply needs. I cannot say with certainty what my mother most deeply needed or whether her unhappiness was the result of a natural defect or a mismatched nurture. I am certain, however, that Grandmother should have been the mother of sons only. If she had been a mother in one of the warlike cities of antiquity, her son would have come back on his shield or carrying it. She could herself have stripped the dead of weapons and finished off the wounded.

Formed by the manners of a softer time, she was never bloodthirsty, and her desire to shine, to triumph over others, was largely confined to canasta and knuckle fights. If it fed her attempt to live a good life, it did not show; her virtue was not ostentatious. One story of battle came down with smiles in the family: her account of racing a stranger in a sleigh on the snow-packed streets of the city because, as she said, she could not let him get ahead of her, could she? The farm had a fast mare in those days and often surprised the city folk when they pulled alongside with their high-stepping animals and fancy rigs.

The third phase of Grandmother's life began not long after the death in 1951 of her brother, Milo, the owner of the farm. Perhaps no one knew it at the time, certainly I did not as I followed Grandmother past the casket in the parlor, but when she paused, touched her brother's hand, and said goodbye, she was saying farewell to a way of life. Ownership passed to her son, my Uncle Sherwin, who, with a wife and two sons, had been living in the second-floor apartment of the farmhouse. What happened in detail I never knew and never heard it discussed as the occasion of acrimony, although the potential was certainly there; but as the next generation came into full possession of the land and business of the farm, it came also into full possession of the house. They moved downstairs. Grandmother was given a choice, a house of her own on the farm or a life with her daughter's family, my family, in a village to the north. After a brief spell as an apartment dweller in the city, she chose my family for reasons I never knew — she may have considered a house an extravagance, she may have felt ousted, she may have thought she could help in a family in which the mother was often incapacitated. Whatever the reason, when I was about sixteen she became a daily presence.

Although her life on the farm was not a job and her departure was not retirement, the transformation was deep and pervasive. She was born on the farm and had lived there all her life except for the brief interval of her marriage. I am tempted to call the move an upheaval except that upheavals are not something Grandmother would have countenanced; she had survived a flood, and if she had been tried by fire, I am sure that whatever the consequences, prolonged agitation would not have been one of them. Given her reticence, it is not surprising that she delivered no speeches on her change of status. To this day I do not know — it is not part of the family lore — whether she grieved for her loss of mastery or felt diminished by the role of second woman. She would not have felt resentment, or not for long. In her most anguished words, her brief allusions to the terrible things her daughter said, she spoke not out of resentment but out of grief. And she did not, I recall, speak as one seeking an ally. She did not engage in factions, think as a partisan, or enjoy the smoke of domestic battle. Profoundly conservative without the zeal of the ideologue, she worked for the common good, as she understood it, in the confines of the life to which she had been called.

She was no stranger to our house and village, where she had visited often. Nevertheless, she must have found it odd to live in a neighborhood where kitchen looked into kitchen and in a house in which the time between visitors was measured in minutes or hours, not days. It was a house in which a normal voice would carry from one end to the other, a house where the pictures and plants were of another's choosing, a house where one could not detect the faint smell of a barn or of fresh warm milk. In the house lived a boy who was discovering girls and who came and went more or less as he pleased, and another woman who, whatever her difficulties, saw the domain as her own and presided over it as best she could. In short, the household gods, though related, were not the same as the ones she had served so long.

There were continuities. She read, sewed, made afghans; the chair by the window in the dining room where she sat every afternoon became known as her rocker. She helped with the meals and the housework, although I suspect that working relations with her daughter were not of the best. And the family of which she was the displaced matriarch remained a family, united, although ever less securely, across generations and marriage lines by sentiment and the slowly dissolving bonds of religion and morality. In the village were many families whose earlier generations had lived on farms, some not so very different from her own. There was no longer the little community chapel, but there was a Congregational church with a regular preacher, deacons, ushers, women's clubs, a flower fund. Grandmother worshiped and found friends there. There were other women of her age who watched an old world start to crumble before corrosive forces, the full power of which would not be seen until they were gone. I wonder if they felt like ancient Romans, their day past, their best energies spent, looking apprehensively beyond the walls to the gathering storm. Grandmother was not a lamenter and did not attract them, so I remember her with her friends, talking, playing cards, attending church functions, unruffled and perhaps oblivious, while their generation and their time passed away.

But this sketch is too passive. Two adventures come to mind which suggest that Grandmother met her later years with more than resilience and stoicism. One is mainly a memory of what other people said, the other something of my own devising and of which I was a beneficiary. Much to the family's surprise, she spent a winter in Florida with a friend and said she enjoyed it. What she did there, how she passed her time, I cannot recall, if I ever knew. The mobile home in which she lived, the shuffleboard she must have watched and perhaps played, the desperate idleness, as I imagine it, of the whole geriatric set loom in my mind as such massive incongruities in the life of this serious woman that I cannot think of the trip as other than a comic misadventure. With her usual reserve, she said it was pleasant, but she did not go back.

The second undertaking I launched myself. No one in my family had ever gone to Europe; indeed, to the best of my knowledge the only relative to that date ever to go overseas was a cousin who had fought at Iwo Jima. Restless at seventeen, sensing that this village was not to be my life, stirred no doubt by romantic stories of adventure, I wanted to work for my passage on a tramp steamer. Either I was not persistent enough or the days of encouraging young adventurers was past, for I could not find a job.

Still eager to go, I turned to Grandmother as what she might have considered an insulting second-best alternative. Even today I wince a little when I think how easy it was for me to ask her to spend her money. I would contribute what I could, but I invited her to make up the difference, the bulk of it, and join me for a summer in Europe. With very little hesitation, she said she would, and we booked a tour. The details are not important, but it is part of her story that she looked on the decadence of the Old World with as much aplomb as she had ruled her little portion of the New, avoiding, it is true, some of the more risqué adventures of the evening, such as the visit to the Folies Bergère or my walks in Pigalle. She did not see, or she ignored, what developed between the handsome French tour guide and the Cincinnati blonde who tickled my back on the beach before discovering that in these matters France was a better teacher than Vermont. But she went energetically and with apparent delight from ship to train to bus, from cathedral to gallery to restaurant, from London to Paris to Rome. We sailed on the *Queen Elizabeth*, on which, to Vermont eyes, even third class was splendid luxury. She was never bored, never sick, never more than normally tired, and she even transcended the deep prejudice of her people to take a sip of wine at my eighteenth birthday party in Geneva. In my younger years, when my worldliness was something to assert and defend, it was with a certain uneasiness that I would admit to having traveled with a grandmother — I would find subordinate clauses to explain or excuse — but in fact I knew I had enjoyed myself, as she had, and I came to relish the memory of the quiet gallantry with which she "did" Europe.

There were other, less dramatic, pleasures — Sunday afternoon rides, church suppers, school music programs, movies, short vacations in Maine, high-school and college graduations. Her normal day was pleasantly and usefully occupied. Other than her one dark confidence, revealing unhappy hours of which this was the only sign, she appeared to live as calmly, as securely, in the knowledge of the good as she had ever done.

Except for the overarching dynamic of the Christian story, the final chapters of which were yet to be written, the world implicit in Grandmother's sense of things was not fluid or progressive. She would have acknowledged material progress and hoped for more, as the founder did in his admiration of the modern plow; but in the things that deeply mattered, the religious and moral life, the object was not to discover, innovate, or transform, it was to conserve and protect. This was not a matter of theory, it was in her bones, and as head of the farm household it was her sacred, if unarticulated, charge. In the village, her opinions did not change; she continued to be the woman she was. Adversity much greater than this gentle usurpation would not have crushed or corrupted her. She could not, however, except in the most indirect ways, resume the guardianship she had lost. Her occupation was gone. More fortunate than many deposed monarchs, she lived out her days in quiet comfort, secure in the knowledge that the next generation welcomed the life she had passed on to it. For me, however, the end of Grandmother's tenure in the farm household was the end of a regime.

Already a traveler, a seeker, I was in the library of a distinguished university when I heard she had died. Like most great modern universities, it encompassed wildly conflicting notions of virtue and excellence and was held together by the single purpose to be the best, leaving the understanding of the best, in its easy democratic fashion, to the wisdom and ambition of its various parts. Grandmother's little unitary world was incongruous there, and I stood as at the hub of some ancient trading center where reckless adventurers could meet and deal, and, out of accident and design, shape the world to come. As I gathered my things and prepared for the trip home, I tried to trace in my mind the road from the provinces that had brought me there. Soon, in a more literal fashion, I was on the road again, homeward bound, to a gathering of the family for the funeral. The organist played an old hymn set to a traditional Irish tune, "Londonderry Air," Grandmother's favorite melody. It is a gentler hymn than one might have supposed, not martial or triumphant but hopeful, touching the heart.

> *Above the hills of time the cross is gleaming,*
> *Fair as the sun when night has turned to day;*
> *And from it love's pure light is richly streaming,*
> *To cleanse the heart and banish sin away.*
> *To this dear cross the eyes of men are turning*
> *Today as in the ages lost to sight;*
> *And so for Thee, O Christ, men's hearts are yearning*
> *As ship-wrecked men yearn for morning light.*

She had died in the hospital, her last words, "I hope I'm not in arrears."

III · The Men

Was it not the farmer that braved the perils of the ocean and sought this Western world that they might enjoy political and religious freedom, that conquered by indomitable energy and perseverance the savage beasts, the savage men, the savage wilderness, and the more than savage clime?

HENRY LESTER, *Man Made for Agriculture*

I went down to Moore's sawmill with Uncle Milo after some boards.

Uncle Sherwin shot a red squirrel out of the elm tree. He blew that little pest all to smithereens. We went up to Mr. Eayres after two hogs. I went up in the corn with Uncle Milo and Clarence.

The men started cutting hay in bridge meadow.

Uncle Sherwin bought me a new cow boy straw hat.

Uncle Milo made me a case for my knife out of a piece of rubber hose.

CHARLES FISH, *Diary Book*

❧

If the household was the heart of the farm, the fields and barns were its back, limbs, and gut. The one was the moral and religious center, the other the economic core, and they supported one another through an ever-flowing exchange of vital nutrients.

It was the men who most obviously carried on the work of the farm, who decided when to plow, when to plant, when to raise up, and when to cut down. It was the men who by cunning and force changed the physical face of things, who broke up the soil, moved rocks, drove fence posts, strung wire, pounded nails, milked cows, spread manure, sharpened knives, slit throats, cut up meat. To me, a boy, this was work as it was most easily apprehended and imitated, even to some degree performed.

Because it took place where they lived, physical work had for me another characteristic: it shaded off imperceptibly into play and moral education so that my uncles in their roles as workers, as teachers, and as companions tended to blend and merge; there were no sharp discontinuities between mending a fence, reminding a boy to do his chores, swimming in the river, and shooting a red squirrel out of a tree. Indeed the very word "roles" would have struck their ears as strange; roles were what Uncle Sherwin and Aunt Ellrena assumed when they put on a play at the community chapel. On the farm the men were who they were and did what they did, and, perhaps to themselves as well as to me, it was all of a piece. Later on, as a traveler looking back, I would call it integration and wholeness, but then it was simply how they lived.

Although they thought of themselves as working, they did not call themselves "workers"; the word would have suggested someone who punched in at a factory. The hired men were hired men and apparently thought of themselves as such, but my uncles

were farmers and what they did was farm. They would say of
someone that he was still "farming it." As is evident in the diary,
the men were always there, sunup to sundown, and what they
did with tractor and plow, hammer and shovel, rifle and knife,
brains and sweat, courage and patience, was for me, the observer
and sometime helper, my earliest schooling in the arts of manhood.

Uncle Sherwin

Beyond the household it was a world of uncles. Three were my
great-uncles, Grandmother's brothers. Milo Lester owned the
farm and worked on it, Henry Lester owned the adjoining farm
across the valley to the west, and Walter Lester lived in a room
at the city hospital where he worked (later he was to live at the
farm). Grandmother's son, Sherwin Williams, lived on the farm
with his wife, Ellrena, and their two sons, Larry and Gareth, and
assumed increasing responsibility as Uncle Milo's health began
to fail. On Sundays all four uncles would sometimes gather to
talk, the tribal elders at their ease with coffee and the Sunday
papers.

Whose voice prevailed in business decisions, I never knew,
but perhaps because he is still alive and active, whereas Uncle
Milo died over forty years ago, Uncle Sherwin is the one I remember as the dominant figure. The diary, in which each appears
almost the same number of times, reminds me that both treated
me as a son and introduced me to the rudiments of their work.
It was Uncle Sherwin who took me along to deliver a load of
wood to the hired man's house when we ran out of gas and had
to putter — "putwer and putwer," the hired man said — to get the
truck started again. It was he who took me to the dairy with the
day's milk or to the hospital to pick up the garbage for the pigs,
he who took me to the summer pasture and let me make the trek
back. The record is sparse, the entries usually matter-of-fact and

unadorned, but their mere presence suggests that what they tell is what mattered. "I rode down with the milk," I wrote, or "Barby and I rode down after the garbage on the back of the truck," or "I walked home from Chittenden about nine miles. We drove down two steers and three cows." Some of the events happened infrequently — herding cows from the summer pasture — but what signified was not their novelty but their understandable purpose and importance, their place in the lives of my uncles, and my opportunity to go along.

Uncle Sherwin is a short man with bandy legs and a rolling gait. As he strode about the farm, he could have been a sailor, the captain or first mate, at ease on the moving deck. Before severe arthritis crippled his legs, requiring first a cane and then a crutch, he moved quickly and purposefully, seeing and hearing everything, attentive to the sounds and movements of animals and machines, quick to notice a cow that moved oddly or an engine that pinged when it shouldn't have. I remember his face — blue eyes, short sandy hair, sunburned skin — on a body never in repose but ever turning, a measured dance in the repetitive tasks of the farm. I remember his strength as he pitched large forkfuls of hay, and his agility as he jumped into the cab of the truck or onto the tractor seat.

Combining energy and command, he was to me not only a master of the world who could drive horses and tractors, herd steers past other people's hayfields, slaughter hogs, milk cows, and castrate piglets, he was also skilled in the more exotic arts of shooting, fishing, and catching wild animals. He "shot a red squirrel out of the elm tree. He blew that little pest all to smithereens." He took a young woodchuck alive, but "the woodchuck was not kept in captivity a great while. He wanted to go back to his hole so he decamped. But we think Mugsy caught him and made a meal out of him." Uncle Sherwin knew how to catch trout, too elusive for me, and he could pick bats out of the air with his shotgun.

To those unaccustomed to rural ways, he may sound like a rough man, but, in fact, he was kind and gentle. I find in the diary that he "put up a swing and we played croqet," and I am reminded of his hearty manner, his clear, direct speech, his almost unfailing good cheer. He would greet a visitor with a "Hello, neighbor!" and make it sound as if it conferred a privileged status. As with many people whose courtesy and affability are especially bracing, there lurked within it the potential for its opposite. As my understanding of these things grew, I came to recognize a spirited nature which had been tamed and civilized by good upbringing and which had the good fortune to be engaged in work that demanded responsibility, decisiveness, action, and vigor. In the heat of the forge, his native force was not weakened but was brought to a fine edge and applied where it was useful; he was well tempered. I recall very few stories of his losing self-control. Once, exasperated, when a young cow did not want to submit to the milking machine and repeatedly kicked off the cups, he bit her on the flank. She stiffened momentarily, then settled down. There was a somewhat darker tale, but hardly a bloody one, of a short fight with a teasing cousin who did not know when to stop. I remember an occasional frown, a hint of impatience in the voice, a sharp reprimand of a child, but no repression and no outbursts in the sense of an unstable bottling up which required periodic uncorkings to ease the heart. In Uncle Sherwin moral nurture had been a discipline, not a muzzle.

The words "moral nurture," however, were probably never used in his family, and abstract or generalized questions of morality, politics, and social change were conveniently encompassed in such comprehensive conclusions as "The times are changing" or "Things always change" and "Things aren't the way they used to be." The details of change, particularly on the practical side of life — such as farming methods and equipment or government farm programs — were often discussed, but the family handled gingerly, if at all, the implications of change for the kind of life they wanted for their children and grandchildren. Allusions, shrugs, a change of inflection, a meaningful silence — these were the signs by which one might read approval or reservations about the course of events. Sharp intellectual debate, the vigorous defense of radical alternatives, would have been foreign and in bad taste.

Having spent much of my life with people who talk about everything, including the things that matter most to them, I must remind myself that with some people a certain reserve is more telling than speech and that conventional words may mask deep yearnings. So it was with Uncle Sherwin, who never preached, but who believed that the work of farming required certain traits of character and, in turn, helped form them, and who not only lived what he believed but tried, with his wife, to pass it on to their sons and, through 4-H, to the sons and daughters of their neighbors. My aunt and uncle were at one in their understanding of the gentle, courteous manner required of family life, and their household on the second floor of the farmhouse was, in many respects, an extension of Grandmother's domain below. If they differed at all with Grandmother, it was not with respect to their fundamental view of life but only in the way, sometimes an important way, that the same convictions and principles are in turn altered — their manifestation is altered — by the peculiarities of the minds and souls, even the bodies, in which they temporarily reside.

At what point the stamp of Grandmother's character began to fade and whether the fainter impression was due to the varying capacities of human nature to receive it or to the powerful bleaching of external forces were not questions that, as a boy, I could have imagined, much less asked. There is no doubt that Uncle

Sherwin saw himself as the heir and guardian of a tradition. No doubt, too, that Aunt Ellrena considered herself co-guardian and was so considered by all who knew her, and if she does not figure largely in this story, it is because for me the woman of the household was Grandmother, and beyond the household was the world of men. While my uncle was more reserved about the moral and religious foundations of family life, it did not mean they had disappeared, although I doubt that in their biblical form they shaped his perception of the world as completely as they did Grandmother's.

Uncle Sherwin's convictions, his sense of guardianship, appeared in his actions. Long a director of the Rutland Fair, a member of the town's planning commission, and about forty-five years a justice of the peace, he believes in self-government and does his part to carry on the work of the town. But it is his work as 4-H leader that I think of most, and there are two references to 4-H meetings in the diary. Seen against the backdrop of more recent notions of pedagogy and child-rearing, the 4-H emphasis on duty, personal discipline, and serving others seems remote indeed. Members of 4-H did not ask that their unique needs be served. They recited the following pledge, as unfashionable now as the founder's admonition that one "must not sigh for the flesh-pots of Egypt" and must cultivate "temperance in all things": "As a 4-H member I pledge my head to clearer thinking, my heart to greater loyalty, my hands to greater service, my health to better living, for my club, my community, and my country."

To my uncle, 4-H's combination of moral, civic, and practical education must have seemed precisely what the farming community needed to perpetuate itself. Having received more formal education than was common for farm youngsters in his day — he was a graduate of the Stockbridge School of Agriculture of the Massachusetts State College at Amherst — he was for over thirty years an informal guide and teacher of the young princes of the blood, the sons and heirs of the local farmers who came to the farm for the regular meetings at which they recited the pledge and learned some of the practical arts of the work which, it was wrongly assumed, they would all end up doing; for over twenty years Aunt Ellrena did the same for the daughters. They, the children, were in fact being trained for a world that ceased to exist, and however useful or healthy the moral lessons they learned, the arena in which they were to exercise them radically changed.

Uncle Sherwin often spoke of change and affected to welcome it or at least to accept it as an inevitability. There were indications however, nuances of tone for the sensitive ear, as well as more tangible evidence, that he was powerfully drawn to the past. On the second floor of the old horse barn, above the shop which sells the vegetables and syrup that in 1965 replaced the dairy business, he assembled a collection of old farm tools which he called his museum. He still likes to pass on memories and family stories about his ancestors; he is a trustee of the town's historical society and helped to produce a collection of stories about the town's past; and he has a keen memory of the farm as it was at various stages of his lifetime.

Of all speech, the kinds hardest to interpret are the most and the least calculated — the most calculated because its author often deliberately casts a veil over his deepest intentions, the least calculated because deep and shallow feelings have equal access to conventional, sentimental utterance. With respect to the past, sentimental utterance was the coin of the realm and was found in the letters, stories, and conversation of the entire family, from grandmother to grandchildren. For Uncle Sherwin such conventional language was the form that reconciled, however imperfectly, the claims of loyalty and affection, a sense of time, a feeling of loss, and the demands of daily life.

Man's craving for signs and wonders, his capacity for high endeavor, and his perverse susceptibility to boredom lead the less anchored souls to underestimate the value of quiet, orderly lives. Although the founder himself urged man to accept his life — "Let him not therefore repine and be unsatisfied with his lot, but cheerfully and industriously submit to act in the sphere for which he was created" — the memory of the nation's birth was fresh in his generation, and he subscribed to a heroic interpretation. It pleased him to say that the patriot-farmers, "for seven long years and on many a bloody field beat and humbled the proud Britons with their mercenary allies. The Europeans fought for the will of a monarch and because fighting was their trade; the Americans fought for liberty in the broadest sense of the word, and it pleased the God of battles to give them finally the victory." The words are predictable, the expansive spirit genuine. The grand gesture, the ringing phrase, the noble deed, the sublime self-sacrifice — these are things that capture the souls of restless men. Echoes of a strenuous and exalted enterprise rang loudly in the ears of the founder. Ambitious, impatient, sometimes harsh, he imagined greatness even as the conditions of his life and the deepest part of his nurture demanded that he apply himself, steadily and repetitively, to daily tasks. The fears and gentle warnings in the letter from his father, Moses Lester — the founder's wife mustn't overdo, their children must receive an appropriate education — and Grandmother's recollection that he was "cantankerous" and "ornery" hint at a certain turbulence in daily life that was calmed by the passing of the generations. His counsel of cheerful and industrious submission was better heeded by his descendants than by himself. Uncle Sherwin's eighty years are a glowing reminder of the utility and grace of a decent life.

Three years after my summer on the farm, however, there occurred a disaster of sufficient magnitude to elevate my uncle to the status of hero. In May 1947 heavy rains broke the flashboards of Chittenden Dam high in the mountains above the farm. From there the water tumbled to East Pittsford Dam, which eventually gave way, sending a cascade down the valley to the farm and the city beyond. Before the dam broke, high water in the pasture had led Grandmother to roll up the rugs and put a few other things out of harm's way. She wanted the family to evacuate, but never before had water come into the house, so not until a phone call told them the dam had broken did they try to leave. Aunt Ellrena, Grandmother, and the two young boys, Larry and Gareth, made it out of the yard, onto the road, and to a neighbor's place on higher ground, but Uncle Sherwin, Uncle Milo, and Clarence Chaffee, the hired man, found themselves in a truck that would not move in the high water that spoiled its traction. The last passerby on the road put Uncle Milo in his car, and his wife drove him to safety. The stranger then helped Uncle Sherwin drag the hired man, now out of his wits with the strangeness of it all, through the water and onto the road, where a neighbor finally rescued them with his truck. The stranger drove off without leaving his name.

These are the episodes of which family legends are made; they met my requirements of decisive action as the mark of heroic virtue. But even as a boy I knew that the heroism was not simply in my uncle's courage, the stranger's rescue, and the presence of mind that braved the flood. It was in the determination, patience, and hard labor that dug out a cellar full of mud; sifted the mud from the first floor to find the ancestral silver teaspoons (all but one); viewed a frog on the kitchen floor and did not despair; cleared away acres of boulders, trees, and other debris; and rebuilt the land, the original, fertile topsoil, fifty-five acres of it, covered by the flood with one to four feet of sand. The blind workings of nature and the frailty of man's contrivances led to a calamity that elevated the decent to the heroic, and completed, for my young imagination, the definition of manhood. It would be years before I could imagine a heroism that was not an expanded version of a man standing firm against great odds, years before I could reflect on the consequences for civic life of the conflict between the need for decent order and the ardent spirit's hunger for distinction, and years before I could entertain the paradox that for the best and worst of men alike, good order is a problem.

The flood left other memories as well. There were pools in the pasture where, with my cousins, I scooped out bullhead. The neighbors reported seeing trees riding upright on the flood as it swept across the farm. The horses were jammed into their stalls by the debris of the flood and when dug out, one of them climbed the stairs to the hay loft where a lone pig had taken refuge. Muggsy, the woodchuck dog, animal hero of the diary, survived to hunt more woodchucks. All the cows were saved by the neighbors who cut a fence to let them escape, but 37 pigs and 188 hens and pullets were lost. The hired man regained his wits and was still hired man four years later when I came to work for the summer. As vivid as my actual memories of Uncle Milo is Grandmother's description of him, looking out at the devastated land from the pantry window, "tears streaming down his face."

Some forty years after the flood, I sat at a meeting with a man from the other side of the state. Exchanging pleasantries, I learned that he once lived in Rutland, that he knew the farm, and that one day in 1947 he and his wife drove out to see the water rise in the valley. They were the last car across the flat and had stopped to help three men struggling against the flood.

The flood was not Uncle Sherwin's alone — I know that now and probably knew it then — but in my picture of the past, he is the hero, courageous and indefatigable, facing death to save others and willing new life into the ruined farm.

He is the last of his generation on either side of my family.

He tended his wife with great care and solicitude in her terrible final illness, and he remains very much at the center of the affairs of the farm, although most of the burden of the operation has passed to his son, Larry, and the business partner, Tim Perry. Sustained by Grandmother's vision, if not so deeply and pervasively governed by it, saved by family habit from dwelling on lost opportunities, untapped talents, and pleasures that might have been, and strengthened by sound business practice, including good products and a rigorous frugality, he remains not only a kind and loving uncle but living proof of the efficacy of prudence, diligence, and integrity. Whatever deep currents, perplexing or otherwise, may have disturbed his felt sense of things as the years passed, his has been, as the world goes, a quiet, prosperous, and fortunate life. If as a traveler I came to hear a different music, it did not deafen me to the notes I first heard as a child, notes that resonate still as I move to an uncertain future.

Uncle Milo

I had three great-uncles, but the one that figured most prominently then and now was the owner of the farm, the one whose "properity," as the diary has it, I was aware of even at that early age. I walked with Grandmother to the boundary of the land and came to know that boundaries mattered. Uncle Milo was owner, and owning conferred a certain distinction that even Uncle Sherwin's daily mastery in the workings of the farm could not completely overshadow. A certain gravity of manner, not unfriendly but slightly formal and reserved, added to the impression of Uncle Milo's stature in the eyes of the world. The farm was known by his last name — it was the Lester Farm — as it had been for two generations before him, and he was the direct descendant of the founder by the male line. Some of this, no doubt, I learned later, but I learned nothing that radically altered my sense of the man as somehow set apart, above not only the common run of humanity but even the other members of the family. Even his bachelorhood and his austere, reclusive habits added to the weightiness of his position, as if, like some priest-king of old, he had been chosen by the gods and must forever bear the mark.

Returning to the diary, I find it odd, although I had never really forgotten it, that this family eminence drove the truck and worked in the barn and fields alongside the rest of the men. In memory he occupies an indistinct borderline between household and field as if in some sense he was lord of both, although Grandmother actually ruled the one and Uncle Sherwin was perfectly capable of ruling the other. Whether it was because he had taken her in or because he represented family or because they enjoyed some natural affinity, he occupied a special place in Grandmother's heart and mind. She conceived of her duties as more comprehensive than service to one person, but if there was a person who embodied for her the to-be-served, it was surely this brother. He was her kind of man. Although she did not bend or cry or pause for more than a moment, her goodbye to him, as she touched his hand in the coffin, is etched in my mind as sharply as any bereavement I have witnessed.

Uncle Milo appears in the diary as frequently as Uncle Sherwin. Not only did he own the farm, he drove to the sawmill for some boards and took me along — a sawmill, by the way, that once whirred and buzzed in the country south of the city, that even a few years ago still stood, an abandoned shack in the path of progress, and that has now disappeared in a wave of restaurants and car lots. Having no children of his own did not handicap him in lending significance to my life. He brought packages of BB's home from the city, he let me help him repair the truck, he "made me a case for my knife out of a piece of rubber hose," he sold my collected papers and magazines for me and brought back $1.65, he "said he might learn me to drive the hay truck," and then, ten days later, "I drove the hay truck . . . We finished the meadow east of the road." Some entries tantalize by what they do not say. I wish I could recall the Sunday when, between Sunday school in the morning and popcorn at night, I walked with Uncle Milo "down by the river." What did we see? What did we say?

There was nothing exceptional about his appearance. Of medium height, sturdy build, with short-cropped, thin, graying hair, a clean-shaven, rather pallid face, a wide, full mouth, and large powerful hands, there was nothing in his physical features to set him off. Since he did in fact stand out in the family and neighborhood, his physical ordinariness must have been a kind of foil to his bearing. He had a gentle manner, but it was measured, not deferential, as if neither to proclaim his presence nor to efface himself. He shared with Grandmother the rare quality of simply being where he was. In some people it is a sign of stolidity, even stupidity, but with them, it was born of knowing who they were, a confidence so rooted they did not need to think about it. Since it never occurred to them they could be dislodged, they needed neither the rigidity of defense nor the agitation of offense to maintain themselves. Without loss of dignity, Uncle Milo could remain silent in conversation or fall asleep in his Boston rocker by the kitchen woodstove. Courteous, not courtly, kindly rather than solicitous, his manner suggested, and his reputation confirmed, a quiet rectitude, steadiness, and probity. He was utterly dependable in things both great and small.

Oddly enough, I cannot remember the sound of his voice, and the only speech I distinctly recall is so out of keeping with the dignity and reserve which remain most clearly in my mind that I hesitate to repeat it. Teaching me to drive the hay truck, that is, how to guide it in first gear across the hay field, he explained the function of the brake pedal by saying you would use it to avoid running into a skunk that might piss on you. Such language never entered the house and even outside was much less common than one might expect. What it signified in this instance, if anything at all, is that Uncle Milo was not only the lofty head of the family but was also a man of the barn and fields.

And so he was, in more fundamental ways. He was known for his physical strength, unusual in a man of his size, and while it was not considered an adequate measure of a man, it was an obvious asset in work as demanding as farming. Ill health, a broken limb, anything that kept a man from lifting and pulling, was not to be taken lightly. Beyond that, he was a "good farmer"; he knew animals, crops, and soils, and he had acquired the arts necessary for their effective management. Known locally for its productivity, the farm could support a cow per acre and yield up to four tons of hay per acre. It is only a slight exaggeration to say that what carries a farm is not the land but the farmer, and certainly Uncle Milo shared with Uncle Sherwin a native spirit-edness, tempered and ordered, that enabled him over a lifetime to govern wisely and firmly. At its lowest, this vitality is a kind of doggedness, a stubborn perseverance, at its highest a disciplined flow of energy, exuberance, and imaginative enterprise. I saw neither extreme in Uncle Milo but rather a steady course over that middle ground occupied by good people, by the virtues of decency, the terrain in which so much of our safety and comfort lies and from which unquiet spirits flee.

Among his four sisters and two brothers as well as the younger generations of the family, he was the patriarch who ex-ercised tangible authority on the farm and a vaguer if still definite influence in the community, as if in some diminished way he kept alive an ancient belief about family continuity and the land. If asked, he would probably have described his understanding of ownership in terms familiar to his fellow citizens in the city and beyond, but there reverberated in the chambers of his heart, as in Uncle Sherwin's, echoes of a long vanished notion of the land as patrimony and legacy rather than commodity. In a city built on the ruins of lost cities beneath it, the ancient patterns and materials survive where utility, necessity, or accident have placed them, but the citizens' most pressing desire is to preserve or extend the realm, not to examine or revive what lies beneath their feet. So in the moral and political realm, the effort is not to articulate the varying strands of experience and feeling but to bind them together in a workable whole. Political necessity demands it, or so men think, and thus a sense of the possibilities of life is lost. It was not in Uncle Milo's calling, as circumstances had shaped it, to examine the roots of his feeling for the farm or to consider if a different order of things would have better fulfilled his nature. He lived the best life he could as it was given him to see it, thereby reenacting the permanent tension between the self-definition of community and the explorations of the roving mind.

An oddity of his life, or so it must have seemed to many, was that he never married. Unmarried men of good family, with a farm and income, were not all that common. That a woman would, through choice or lack of opportunity, live out her days as a spinster, either alone or with another woman, struck no one as strange, but believing that men's needs were more compelling than women's, people were often surprised to hear of an eligible lifelong bachelor. And many bachelors were not eligible, that is, they were the drifters, the chronically unemployed or underemployed, or the neighborhood eccentrics, men so odd that either they did not need women or reasonable women would not have them. Normal, healthy men needed women, even if the need and its satisfaction were not as crudely advertised as today. The family never offered an explanation for Uncle Milo's single state, although they seemed to feel, without ever quite saying so, that it added a certain power or efficacy to his position, just as celibacy does to that of a priest. It seemed to be of a piece with his reclusiveness, his apparent self-sufficiency, his wish to stay on the farm and to keep his own counsel. It was said of him that he never wanted to go anywhere—to fairs or meetings or social gatherings—but that when he went he had a good time. He had to be coaxed.

As far as I know, he lived a celibate life, never courted anyone, never fell in love. The only hint that he may have felt more than brotherly or neighborly affection for a woman was his legacy to a former housekeeper who had looked after him and the house when Grandmother was ill. Although not a large sum of money, it was too large to be a mere token of remembrance, and I recall my parents' guarded speculation when the will was read. In the indiscriminate celebration of erotic fulfillment that characterizes our time, it is hard to understand his celibacy as anything other than an unfortunate loss, something fundamental missing in his life. And indeed it may have been precisely that.

As I think my way back into this lost time, however, as I examine the elements of life and then imagine the whole, I see a cluster of interlocking patterns, no one perfect or complete, but making together a workable family and community. Judged as it is today the fashion to judge, almost exclusively in terms of individual achievement and satisfaction, these lives may seem sharply circumscribed. Although the notion of pleasure or growth outside the family was not beyond their ken and there were, of course, people who moved away and took jobs, there was a sharp difference between moving away because that is where the job was and moving away into a radically different set of expectations for life. Without ever talking about it, perhaps without even thinking about it very much, Uncle Milo lived for the family and the farm, and I imagine that whatever limitations this devotion and the peculiarities of his birth and nurture may have imposed upon him, whatever satisfactions they may have denied him, his life thus defined made sense to him and was good.

The goodness was felt by others, too, although not by all. When he died, my parents inherited enough money to pay off the mortgage on their house. I learned that Uncle Milo had done many kind deeds over the years, unsung but not unappreciated, helping neighbors in his quiet way. A niece who received little or nothing was angry, however, and let it be known, a dramatic gesture in a family with a deep aversion to open hostility.

His goodness, in fact, was a given in the family's understanding of itself, so much so that on one unhappy occasion when my mother and father were arguing about sin, my mother in her anxious way saying that all people are sinful and my father more casually reserving the word for grand offenses, it was my father's rhetorical inspiration to ask, "Well, what about Uncle Milo? Has he sinned?"

When his last illness grew on him and he needed constant attention, my mother went to the farm to help Grandmother and Aunt Ellrena care for him. When the phone call came to say he had died, my father put my brother and me in the car and headed south. Because of the coincidence of things, the irrelevant attaches itself with indecorous abandon, and I will always associate Uncle Milo's death with the automobile accident on the trip to the farm, the squeal of tires, the helpless drift, the crunch of the impact, and the vehemence of my father's brother, a peppery man who surveyed the damage and said of the driver of a third vehicle, which caused the accident, "The son of a bitch, the son of a bitch!" Uncle Milo's mind went before his body, and although the time was short, I found it sad that this dignified and private man had to be nursed like a baby in his final days. He died in his sixty-eighth year in the house in which he was born, the third generation of his line to own and work the farm, honored and loved by those who knew him and remembered still.

Uncle Bub

Walter Lester, Uncle Bub, was the great-uncle who had only one arm. He had two actually, but one had been withered by polio and hung at his side. One leg was crippled, too, and he wore a special heavy shoe with a brace and walked with a cane. Misfortune had plagued him in other ways as well: a wife who died young, a farm he found difficult to manage (it adjoined Uncle Milo's farm across the river to the south), and, after the farm, a very ordinary job. If he had measured happiness by his portion of the goods men clamor for, he would have been profoundly unhappy. Fortunately, he did not.

Seeing him after an absence, I would notice first the shriveled arm, helplessly swinging if not stuffed in a pocket, then the slow, painful gait, and finally the thick glasses with their heavy frames dark against the thin, gray hair and the pink skin that shone as if freshly scrubbed. On the face there was always a quizzical, ironic smile, as if life had just presented him with a delightful curiosity, some oddity to please and amuse.

When I went to the hospital with Uncle Sherwin to pick up the garbage for the pigs (the richest imaginable garbage since it was the patients' uneaten food), Uncle Bub came out of the boiler room where he was the fireman and with his one good arm slung the barrels around the little room in which they were stored. There was always a smile, a hearty greeting, and it did not strike me as odd that this descendant of a landowning family should be so employed.

He had two children, a daughter and a son. Carley was to me an indistinct figure, a tall, slender woman with a full mouth and a sweet smile; her voice lives in my mind in a certain inflection, a cadence, like a bar or two of an otherwise forgotten song. Harlan, on the other hand, loomed large in my imagination and is still vivid. He may have been a bit of a roughneck, if family allusions meant what they seemed to (tough as a boiled owl, my father said), and I never thought of him as in any way under the control of his father or, in fact, as having any special connection with him beyond the mere fact of parentage. But that was beside the point and of no interest. What was of intense interest was the fact that he had joined the Marines, forging his father's signature for approval to enlist at seventeen, and had fought in the Pacific war, landing with the third wave on Iwo Jima and returning unscathed with Japanese souvenirs and carefully censored stories of terrible deeds. Later I would see him at the farm and hear of his exploits. He represented the manly side of those early years in its most natural form: his cunning, zeal, and courage in war; his love of hunting and fishing; his capture of raccoons and woodchucks, which he kept in cages on the farm; his dark good looks, handsome smile, and booming laugh; his physical strength and powers of endurance. Hit by a car before he joined the Marines, he lay in a coma for twenty-one days, and for a long time the doctors, who thought he was doomed, dared not touch him, fearing that any disturbance would kill him. The newspapers reported that there was no hope for him; his father picked out a coffin. He survived.

Perhaps that was the link with his father, the refusal to quit. In Uncle Bub, endurance became graceful, an ornament of the spirit and a blessing to those who knew him. In fact, it ceased to be endurance, which is, after all, a virtue of horses and mud turtles as well as men, and became a kind of energetic cheerfulness, all the more charming in that it had not a trace of adversity overcome, no gritting of the teeth. I remember a flow of humorous observations and quips, the kind that do not repeat well because they are the overflow of temperament, not independent jokes or stories. The supper table was the merrier for his presence.

Without speeches or any show of virtue, Uncle Bub also made himself useful. As the diary notes, he helped me dig a woodchuck out of a stone wall. In later years he came to live at the farm, where I often saw him repairing things or hoeing the garden or even sweeping the kitchen floor, using his one good arm and, with surprising efficiency, foot, knee, or hip to get the job done. At retirement age, no doubt unemployable and with very little money, lame and handicapped, he had become a dependent and today would belong to a politically definable class, the physically challenged or the differently abled or whatever the current euphemism is. Ironically, in his refusal to think of himself as handicapped, he lent substance to the euphemisms—he rose to the challenge, he was "abled"—and it is hard to believe that he would have done better if he had been more the object of social concern. He was fortunate, however, in his disposition and nurture and in the accident of birth into a family who had the means to care for him and the wit and heart to respond to his own fine spirit. If he ever considered himself a dependent—he may have, he was the least confessional of men—he never let on, nor was he ever so described by anyone in the family. The family loved him, he brightened the day, and when the time came, they took him in, not because they had to but because they wanted to.

It is impossible to know precisely the constituent parts of Uncle Bub's remarkably buoyant temperament. Lacking such precise knowledge, I can only say that he was well served by the family blend of loyalty, affection, and austerity into which he was born. Either a harsher or a softer regime might have made an emotional as well as a physical cripple of him, the one producing bitterness instead of sweetness, the other melting his resolve and encouraging self-pity.

The blend that served his character so well achieved its goal partly by imposing limits, by setting the course and sticking to it. Who knows what seeds of reflection may have sprouted and died in the mind of this hearty, resolute man, what peculiar perspectives on the world might have been generated by his condition if such speculations had been encouraged? It is our fate to live but once and that in a certain way.

Uncle Henry

Most remote of the three great-uncles, despite his physical proximity, was Henry Lester, who owned the adjoining farm across the valley to the west and who bore the name of the founder. In appearance and manner he was what the word "avuncular" calls to mind — white-haired, pink-cheeked, slow-moving, jolly, and stout, a veritable Santa Claus of a man, most distinctly present in my memory, however, not standing by a chimney but sitting at the kitchen table on the farm at one of the Sunday morning gatherings.

He had rimless glasses which slid down his nose and, it seemed to me, a perpetually smiling face that lacked the sprightliness of Uncle Bub's cheerful countenance. He was affable and accommodating; I have heard it said that he could get along with anyone. I know little of his domestic fortunes except that he had one child, a daughter. I know I am forging a pattern out of the slightest of materials, but in Uncle Henry's manner and in what I recall of the farm I imagine a lack of vigor. His house, barn, and land were poor compared to the valley farm with its fine buildings and rich, flat fields. The buildings seemed both old and impermanent, doomed but surprisingly tenacious, clinging to the sloping land like a burr on a dog rather than sinking deep roots into the earth as the valley buildings gave the illusion of doing.

What I sensed in the hillside farm was a lack of determination to impress one's will upon the land, although I should add that, given the economics of modern farming, it is unlikely that any combination of skill and determination could have saved it. Farmers may love their land and farms (some no doubt do not), but it is a demanding love, requiring great energy and unremitting attention, for the elements with which the farmer works — land, plants, animals, buildings, machines — will all revert to an unproductive natural form without the constant ordering of the farmer's art. Either that or the farm will succumb to what is known as a higher use, one yielding a greater financial return. Uncle Henry is long gone, as is the hillside farm, now put to the higher use of the homes and playgrounds of the successful (doctors, lawyers, merchants, perhaps a thief or two, but no Indian chiefs), whose talents and ambitions are more in tune with the age in which they live. Drawn to the country for reasons of the heart they may not understand, they owe their best energies, their training, and their self-respect to the city where they work. For better or worse, home and work are separated, as are the lives of parents and children; eight-year-olds now play where once they would have herded cows.

The Hired Men

I can think of eight of them, either men I have known or ones who came down in family stories from the time of my mother's childhood. For reasons worth pondering, most memories of them are amusing. Clarence Chaffee appears in the diary as the man who took me fishing one day, and he was still working on the farm seven years later when I returned for the summer as a hired man myself. Even small boys addressed hired men by their first names. Clarence stayed at the farm except for every other weekend when he visited relatives, and he was never known to take a bath, yet he did not smell. Not the most energetic worker, he probably sweated less than some people, but in July and August one would sweat lying down, and still he did not smell. The world beyond the farm and the city was mysterious to him, but once, when young, he went out West. Where out West, someone would ask. The answer was Albany (New York) and it was not a joke. Another hired man was from Poland and pronounced "sheets" as "shits," which caused no end of amusement. Another looked like poor Judd from *Oklahoma*, never smiled, and was said to have a succession of women, which gave him a certain aura of outlawry. When I was in college, riding home from the Midwest with a friend, I had an accident at a traffic light in Rutland. The other driver was the many-womaned hired man; he did not want to summon the police. Another man was married, lived nearby, and was blind in one eye. Having done so well with only one, he had a certain arrogance about the visible world and would back his car without looking onto the busy road, trusting that others would give way.

Not all stories of the hired men are amusing, though. A man of mysterious origin, cultivated and well spoken, played the piano beautifully and gave lessons to Uncle Sherwin and Aunt Ellrena's younger son, Gareth. One day he dropped dead in the barn, an event probably no more astonishing to him, if he had time to ponder it, than the fact that he was there at all.

If a hired man lived on the farm, he slept in a small room on the second floor of the house, took his meals with the family, and received a modest wage. (This was a change from the founder's era when, as Grandmother wrote, "help was very cheap; often board and tobacco would pay them, and, I suppose, cider thrown in.") Whatever his habits off the farm, a man was expected to maintain a certain decorum on it, especially in the house and at table. He worked long hours as all farmhands did, but he was not expected to work harder than my uncles and he was not singled out for the nasty or more tedious jobs.

Given the equality of working conditions and a certain affection that developed over time, the men who stayed the longest might be said to become part of the family. In Grandmother's scrapbook, under a photograph of Clarence Chaffee, I find this caption in her hand: "A typical 'real' hired man. Faithful, honest, trustworthy. One of the family. Worked for Uncle Milo and Sherwin a good many years." Certainly the men were treated considerately and much of the time a visitor could not have told by tone of voice whether a family member was speaking to another family member or to the hired man. But if hired men were family, it was in a most limited sense. The connection was, of course, fundamentally economic. The man needed an income, food, a place to stay, and the farm needed a hand. Unlike the dependents of slavery or serfdom, the man was free to leave, and the close physical proximity, the working conditions, and the family's customary civility rendered the economic tie less soulless than, say, factory work, the paradigmatic employment of modern, democratic capitalism. (Perhaps now it's the office worker at the computer keyboard.) There was room for a certain amount of initiative, for the development of skills in working with machinery and animals, and for the assumption of greater responsibility. Some hired men could be relied upon to do the milking unsupervised, some could not.

There was no room for significant advancement, however. The farm at that time was, so to speak, a closed corporation, and it was unlikely that anyone who would be willing to do such work for this pay would be the kind of person who could eventually become a partner in the business, even if the business could use a partner. (Times change; the business dimension of the farm is now in a partnership with an able man from outside the family.) The position tended to attract the eccentric or those outside the mainstream for any number of reasons. The farm was like many others in this respect. It offered not a career but a reasonably secure berth, short- or long-term, to those who needed it and could do the work. Over the following generation, many farms saw the professionalization of the hired man, the demand for higher wages, shorter hours, benefits. Whereas the man was once something like a retainer in an extended family, he now took a job. Whether it was a gain or a loss depends on one's estimation of the relative importance of independence, affection, security, and money.

When the time came for moral exhortations about work, for hearing folk wisdom reduced to epigrams and other simplicities, I had seen the context in which they made sense. I had seen the work of men as an unquestioned daily necessity. I had begun to understand, although I could not have explained, the peculiar intimacy of work and character, related as the making of music is to the musician's trained ear. And I had glimpsed, in gentle form, the inescapable hierarchy of human interactions.

IV · Work

. . . but the subtlety of the serpent and the beauty of the fruit was too much for a person of Mother Eve's construction. She ate and persuaded the man to do likewise, and for this transgression of our first parents, they were sentenced to be agriculturists, in the sweat of their face to eat their bread.

For this increase in production, we may look to the greater intelligence of the present generation, the study of agriculture as science.

HENRY LESTER, *Man Made for Agriculture*

I am still sprouting my potatoes.

I drove the hay truck for Uncle Milo today. We finished the meadow east of the road.

I have started to feed the hens today.

The men started puting hay in the horse barn and I called off for the men.

I went to Chittenden today. I helped get the miserable old cattle back in where they belong. We fixed the fence up in Chittenden.

I walked home from Chittenden about nine miles. We drove down two steers and three cows.

CHARLES FISH, *Diary Book*

It was the farm's summer I knew best, the long days, the sun, the labor in the fields. I saw the daily cycle, the repeated chores, the evolving pattern of the season, the irregular elements that floated within the constant frame. I did not see the larger cycle, the pattern of the year.

True cycles have no beginning or end, but the farm measured things by seedtime and harvest, birth and death, and it would be reasonable to start with spring. Spring planting, however, was preceded by fall plowing, most of it in October. To break the soil, my uncles used a red FARMALL tractor, four years old that summer, the first tractor the farm ever had and the first rubber-tired tractor in the neighborhood, pulling a moldboard plow that could be raised and lowered hydraulically and could be turned to throw the furrow right or left. For years horse-drawn moldboard plows had turned the soil, the earth curled over and smoothed shiny brown by the concave fold of the blade. It was the horse-drawn version of this plow that the founder praised as "the first of agricultural instruments now in use." As much as that of Robert Fulton, "let the name of Joseph Nourse be remembered as benefactor of his race for bringing the plow to its present perfection." One form was the sulky plow on which the farmer rode, another the handle plow guided by a man walking behind a horse, repeating in its essentials a pattern stretching back to antiquity. The first tractor-drawn plow, like its predecessors, cut a single furrow; later the farm would use three-furrow plows, big farms five. Since the land was flat or gently sloping, my uncles did not need to plow in contours to prevent erosion and could rely instead, in the sloping big rock meadow, on strip plowing, which left a narrow strip of grass every seventy-five feet or so. They plowed the long way of the fields to minimize turning. As the fresh soil curled over, insects and worms appeared, and soon blackbirds and crows would follow the tractor. Many years later, sea gulls appeared, miles from any large body of water.

Unlike some modern tractors used in the West, the FARMALL had no cab and my uncles sat exposed to the sun and rain. Cranking the engine by hand to start it, they first made sure the transmission was in neutral, for a strong man could start an engine in gear and find himself crushed against the barn wall. Careful men held the thumb and fingers on the same side of the crank handle and exerted the most force on the upward pull, for if the handle kicked back it could break a straddling thumb or dislocate the shoulder of an arm extended straight on a downward push.

After plowing, the land was left till spring, except for manuring (in the winter, when the cows were inside, the barn was cleaned daily). Unlike the farms along Lake Champlain with their treacherous clay soil, this farm had silty loam, which does not hold the water long, and in the spring, as soon as it was dry enough to work, it was harrowed, first with a tractor-drawn wheel harrow with sharp rotating disks, and then with a smoothing harrow, also known as a spring-tooth, which clawed the soil with metal fingers and left it fine enough for planting.

There were two main crops in those days, both for cattle: corn, which was planted about Decoration Day (Memorial Day), and hay, which was seeded in the corn at the time of its last cultivation (weeding), in late June. The corn would shade the young grass shoots, and for the following three or four years the field would produce a hay crop until, in rotation, corn would be planted once more. Corn depletes the soil, so a field would have corn for one year, hay for three or four.

The hay was seeded with a wheelbarrow seeder, a box about twelve feet long, mounted over a wheel and pushed by hand across the field. The machine with its wheel-drive mechanism dropped the seed with commendable evenness, and in two days, between morning and evening chores, a man could seed ten to twelve acres, but it was hard to push. Uncle Sherwin and Larry still remind me that when I returned to the farm to work, I painted the words "Blood, sweat, and tears" on the box.

Corn planting was more elaborate. A horse-drawn plank with skids for markers crossed the field first one way, then the other, in a checkerboard pattern. Where the skid lines intersected was where one planted. The planter was a hand-held corn stabber, a stick with an attached box which held the seed corn, and a mechanism beneath, which dropped about six kernels into one hill when the point was stabbed into the ground and moved back and forth. Uncle Sherwin says the six kernels were accounted for by the old rhyme:

> *One for the blackbird,*
> *One for the crow,*
> *One for the cutworm,*
> *And three to grow.*

The hills were three feet apart. As with seeding hay, a man could cover ten to twelve acres in two or three days between chores. It was hot work, but Uncle Milo could work two stabbers at the same time. Now the farm plants sweet corn for its market garden with a tractor-drawn planter.

The tractor signaled a great change in the operations of the farm, but horses were still used for cultivating, drawing the weeder and hay wagons, raking hay, and sugaring. When I returned to the farm as a hired man in 1952, the horses were gone.

One plot of land in the field to the north of the house, near the flower garden, was reserved for vegetables — prepared, planted, and weeded by the men, but picked mainly by the women. In those days vegetables were grown for home use, not for sale, and they included the standard fare, with none of the exotics which appear on the cooking pages of glossy magazines. I remember radishes, lettuce, Swiss chard, cabbage, carrots, string beans, summer squash, tomatoes, corn, pumpkins, and blue Hubbard squash. Each year 200 pounds of seed potatoes were planted in a separate plot, changed yearly to minimize the danger of blight and to reduce witchgrass. When I returned to the farm to work, one of my jobs was dusting potatoes with the insecticide rotenone, spread with a green, hand-cranked duster carried over the shoulder. I was proud when Grandmother remarked that I moved through the patch much faster than the regular hired man. Although the farm could have bought what it needed, growing one's own was the customary way of providing vegetables, and many townspeople, only a generation off the farm, carried on the practice as well. Important as it was in the domestic economy of the farm, the garden was different from the fields. To work in it was not the same; it was a shade or two closer to recreation or pleasure, standing at some intermediate point between growing hay and growing flowers.

The seasons affected births, but as much for the convenience of man as out of the necessities of nature. More piglets were born from spring to early fall than in the winter. Baby chicks were bought in the spring and would begin to lay at five or six months. Cows freshened (gave birth) any time, but a more or less uniform spacing around the calendar was desirable because it evened out milk production. Extra calves in the spring were undesirable, for this was when the cows were turned out to feed on the fresh green grass, which increased milk flow; as volume rose, prices fell.

Spring flowed into summer. Hay required little attention once it was planted, corn needed regular cultivating during June until it was too tall, and the garden was weeded in part every few days and dusted as needed. To cultivate corn, Uncle Milo or Uncle Sherwin guided a horse-drawn, hand-held cultivator between the rows to kill weeds and break up the soil for better moisture retention. The cultivator had three sets of teeth, one behind the other, that could be set to cover a narrower or wider area. Now farms control weeds mainly by herbicides.

The main summer job was haying. When it was time for the first cutting, usually about July 1, the men kept one eye on the ripening grass, waiting for full bloom on the timothy and clover, and one eye on the sky, hoping for good weather. A blue sky, bright sun, and dry air made for good haying. "Good haying weather, isn't it?" was the greeting, and someone might even say, "Well, we better make hay while the sun shines." There was sometimes a smaller second cutting called rowen. My uncles liked to finish haying by the end of July, but bad weather could postpone it.

Hay was not just dead grass. Hay was what Uncle Sherwin fed the cows to make them give a lot of milk. And so it was true, in a sense, that the farmer *made* hay — choosing certain seed and not others, preparing the soil, harvesting at the right moment — and its making was a subordinate art under the more comprehensive art of farming. Hay for the farm was not just one species of grass; it was a mixture of timothy, redtop, medium red clover, and alsike (a clover with a red and white blossom). For two years the clover would be strong, then fade as the timothy took over. In wet fields, my uncles sometimes planted reed canary grass and

broom grass. Alfalfa, later widely used, required special soil preparation and was uncommon at the time.

It was agricultural research scientists who worked out the
combination, along with the advantages of hybrid corn and the
efficacy of pesticides and fertilizers, at the great schools around
the country, nearly all in land-grant institutions provided by the
government a century before to meet the practical needs of a
growing nation. Following ancient authority, the founder might
say that as a result of man's fall, "the ground was accursed and
to ever produce thorn and thistles," but from deeper within him,
in contradiction, sprang a grateful recognition of God's bounty
and an optimistic faith in progress. Agricultural research was the
implementation of his belief in "the greater intelligence of the
present generation," his conviction that successful farming required the "study of agriculture as science, the study of chemistry,
the analyzing of plants." By such lifelines of support and depen-
dency, the body and guts of the farm were bound to the great
world of science, technology, and invention. And by analogous
links its heart and soul were fed not only by its most immediate
beliefs but by some of the principles and motives of the larger
society. It was this particular mix of beliefs, principles, and motives that gave the farm its individual character and that contained
the seeds of its transformation, moving it closer to the rhythms
and opinions of the outside world.

The hay was ready to cut when little green was left. If too
dry, it was said to be drier than a muslin fart. If too green, it
could spontaneously ignite in the barn from the heat generated
by moisture and pressure under its great weight. This farm had
been spared the calamity, thanks to my uncles' care, but I had
stood by at other barn fires, and I knew that the stakes were high.
I had seen a burned horse led from a barn and repeatedly and
clumsily shot until it died.

When the hay was ready, Uncle Sherwin connected the mowing machine to the power take-off at the rear of the tractor. The machine had a steel cutter bar of sharp triangular teeth, which slid rapidly back and forth over an identically shaped stationary bar, clipping the hay in the triangular notches as the machine moved forward across the field. It cut the hay; it also cut nesting birds, mice, and any animal that happened to get in the way. Every farm had three-legged cats from time to time. In good weather Uncle Sherwin could mow a stand of hay one day, rake it the next, and draw it to the barn the third. Raking aerated the hay and gathered it in long rows called windrows. The horse-drawn side delivery rake had ground-driven rows of teeth, mounted at an angle to the forward motion, which would pick up the hay and deliver it to one side in a neat, continuous row. Scatterings were gathered with a horse-drawn dump rake, which was mounted at right angles to the line of motion and was raised or "dumped" periodically to form sections of a windrow.

With the hay now in windrows, the men would attach a hay-loader to the rear of a wagon pulled by horses. About six feet wide and ten feet tall, it leaned above the bed of the wagon. Raker bars (push bars) picked the hay off the ground and up the bed of the loader to the top, where it dropped to the wagon floor. One of my uncles would drive while the other, or a hired man, with a three-tined pitchfork would place the hay around the wagon to make a balanced load.

When the wagon was full, it was taken to the gable end of the barn under a metal track that projected at ridge level out of the loft. The big barn, the stable, and the horse barn each had a loft and the same system for picking up the hay. Attached to the track by pulleys and a release mechanism was a grapple fork with four curved prongs resembling scimitars or scythe blades but with sharper arcs, each prong about three feet long and hanging loose so that it could be placed as the eye of the man judged best.

Plunged into the hay at appropriate intervals according to its layering, the fork would lift a large load. Four hitches, as they were called, would empty a wagon. Someone, preferably a boy who was not otherwise useful, would stand where he could be seen both by the man on the wagon and by another man at the other end of the barn who, with tractor or horses, would pull the load by ropes and pulleys up to the track at the ridge and along it to the place in the loft where a man with a pitchfork was carefully and sweatily stacking it. This man would yell "Whoa!" when the load reached the right point. The boy, who could hear the "Whoa," had to "call off," that is, shout or signal to tell the man who was doing the pulling when to stop. Some men had good lungs and might have made the boy's job unnecessary. Uncle Sherwin can remember hearing "Whoa" from the hired man on Uncle Henry's farm across the valley. The man on the load would release the fork from the track with a trip rope, dropping the load into the mow, and would then pull the fork back up to the track and along it to the end, where it would descend for another hitch. Meanwhile, in the loft, the man with the hottest, dustiest job mowed (rhymes with "cowed") the hay away with a pitchfork in such a fashion that he could retrieve it easily when needed. Despite appearances, hay in a pile does not consist of uniform units that can be handled indiscriminately like sand or sawdust; rather, it gathers in layers that can bind like logs or sheets of fabric and can be easily disassembled only in the reverse order of its composition. In his museum over the shop in the old horse barn, Uncle Sherwin has a hay saw, a coarse-toothed blade for cutting hay that was badly bound.

What I glimpsed that first summer became vivid to me when I returned as a hired man: materials have their individual natures, and he who would work with them successfully must first understand them. This was true not only of hay but of animals, both species and individuals, and eventually I came to wonder about human beings and their multifarious development in political societies. My uncles and my grandmother understood the materials with which they worked, they knew the ends for which they handled them, and they had learned the art by which the one could be made to serve the other. Somewhere in their feelings about life, most visible perhaps in Grandmother, existed the belief that beyond this art, the ends and means so clearly articulated, there were other ends, ultimately compelling and determinative but harder to serve because less clearly understood. Into such obscure regions I was later to venture, first as I struggled into manhood and later as I traveled beyond the boundaries of family, farm, and village.

Cutting the corn came much later, not until the first or second week of September. The corn harvester, pulled by horses, cut one row at a time, tied eight to ten stalks in a bundle, and tossed the bundles to one side. The bundles were drawn on flat wagons to the silo, which was attached to the big barn near the stable ell. There a man fed the stalks into a corn blower, which chopped them into pieces one to two inches long and blew them up a tube to the top of the silo, where they gradually filled the interior and were known in this condition as ensilage or silage, that which has been ensiled (the verb was never used on the farm). Weather mattered much less, for with its heavy moisture content the corn was not damaged if harvested in the rain. And there was no danger of fire, for although heat built up in the corn under the massive weight of the finely packed ensilage, the result was fermentation which preserved it. Deadly gases were emitted, but this old silo was well enough ventilated to prevent their accumulation.

Of the two common kinds of corn at that time, flint corn, which matured early, and dent corn, which was later but more resistant to borers, my uncles preferred dent. They wanted to cut

it before frost and at the dent stage, when the kernels began to
dent or shrivel. Flint corn was cut when the kernels were hard
or just before, at the hard-dough stage.

With the corn in the silo, the two major tasks of the summer
and early fall were done. Work went on, but August and September was a time of fairs, and Rutland Fair in those years drew
more people than any other in the state. For the town family, the
fair was mainly amusement, girlie shows to auto racing, with the
agricultural exhibits curiosities only or, for those not long off
the farm, sentimental reminders of a way of life they had left. The
farm family was drawn by the same amusements, but the agricultural dimension, once the primary purpose of the institution
and now losing out to the carnival atmosphere, remained significant. According to Grandmother, the founder was one of the men
who introduced fairs locally, first one-day stock shows, then
longer and more elaborate events. I suspect that the fairs descend
from old-world harvest festivals, and that the 4-H boys and girls
(and their parents, too) who exhibited their livestock, vegetables,
baked goods, and canning were only the most recent participants
in an ancient custom that in some essentials remained unchanged
even as it was transformed to meet new needs and hopes.

In my time, much of the activity assumed a continuity between the generations that events were to frustrate. The 4-H
members were honored not as children doing childlike things but
as future men and women learning the arts of farming and farm-
household management. Some of them stayed the week at the
fair, sleeping in the barns with the animals, feeding and grooming
them for show. Farm-equipment dealers displayed shiny new tractors, wagons, manure spreaders. Farm families who may not have
seen each other for months could meet and talk. For some families,
it was the major outing of the year, a relief from work but not
detached from it. As a director of the Rutland Fair, Uncle Sherwin

felt he was performing a public service. In time his son Larry, who had been superintendent of the poultry barn, would succeed him as director and his grandson Paul would be in charge of the vegetables. Larry watched over the productive varieties of chickens and turkeys but also a surprising array of exotic fowl, including some whose breeding and bearing showed that they were intended to provide neither eggs nor meat but illegal excitement in the pit.

Fall was a time for miscellaneous repairs of tools and equipment that would be used the following year. It was also the time to draw sawdust from a local mill to fill the bins in the big barn, from which it was spread under the cows to provide bedding and absorb urine. In October my uncles plowed. The longest job was cutting wood, which went on, although not steadily, from November to spring. The house furnace used wood, as did the fire for boiling maple syrup. From the sugar bush my uncles culled other species that had sprung up, mainly beech and yellow birch, and the occasional maple that had blown over or was dying. Working before chain saws, they felled trees with a two-man crosscut saw, each man cutting on the pull stroke in a rhythmic exchange. With horses and chains they skidded the logs, three or four to a hitch, out of the woods, down the hill, and across the flat to the back of the house, where they cut them to length with an electric reciprocating saw, winching them by hand along a track into cutting position. They split the chunks by hand, using an ordinary axe and, for tough pieces, wedges and a maul; they did not have splitting mauls or power splitters. Limb wood and slabs from the sawmill they cut to length with a circular saw driven by a belt from the tractor's power take-off; most of this wood went to the sugarhouse.

In winter the cows were let out of the barn and into the barnyard for only an hour and a half or so in the morning to give the men a chance to clean the stable and observe which cows were coming into heat; if they would stand still when mounted by other cows, they were ready for breeding. In the barn the manure accumulated rapidly. It was before the days of in-ground manure pits or slurry tanks, and the manure was spread directly on the fields every day. When I worked on the farm, a newfangled barn cleaner had been installed, an electrically powered moving chain with attached bars, which ran in a loop around the barn through the gutter (a trench about a foot wide and eight inches deep) behind the cows and up an incline to the outside where the manure it had been pushing dropped into a manure spreader. In my first summer on the farm, the litter carrier was still in use, a tub about three feet wide by four feet long and two feet deep, attached by chains and pulleys to an iron track which ran around the ceiling of the stable above the gutter. The bucket could be lowered, filled with a shovel, pushed to the next location, and finally raised to the track, pushed outdoors, and inverted by a trip release over the spreader. The spreader was a tractor-drawn wagon with a wide ground-driven belt for its bed. When engaged the bed would move backwards, carrying the manure into rapidly rotating teeth which would spread it in a wide pattern across the field. In the coldest part of winter the wet manure would freeze in the spreader, so a sled or old wagon was used instead and the manure was spread by hand. If spread soon after it was collected from the barn, it would steam in the cold winter air. I carry in my mind to this day a picture of a distant tractor and spreader, a hunched driver, wisps of vapor rising, and, to the rear, the scattered brown stains on the snowy ground. The tractor moves slowly, its gentle chugging the only sound, and for an instant man and machine become as natural a part of the landscape as the frozen field itself or the leafless trees beyond.

They are natural, of course, only to the naturalizing human

eye, which deceives the mind and heart and sees the familiar as if it were granted by Mother Nature herself and not by a collaboration supervised by the arts of man. To the city boy, sidewalk and alley are as natural as woods and streams to his country cousin, and if the latter enjoys any superiority in the matter, it is only that he is less likely to ignore the thought and effort required to make a human environment; he sees more clearly what there is without it. And so in the fall and winter, my uncles battled the destructive forces of nature, just as in the summer they drew on her powers of generation. For what man has joined together, nature wants to put asunder, reducing the contrivances of art to their useless elements through abrasion, rust, decay, pressure, and frost. There were harnesses to mend, tools to repair, here a broken shovel handle, there a worn tire or a cranky engine.

Perhaps even more demanding is the art of cultivation today. The most sophisticated and far-reaching efforts of science come to its aid; genetic engineering finds some of its most obvious applications in agriculture. Now, years off the farm, I think of the arts of justice by which my forebears had devised various political associations in the light of their conceptions of God's plan or the nature of things, guiding toward the common good those powers of the soul which, improperly or inadequately cultivated, were the rust and decay of the body politic. If there is a devil, he must chuckle at the spectacle of a world in which some of the finest minds attend to the perfection of corn while the cultivation of souls is left to the muses of the marketplace.

The bridge from winter to spring was sugaring, the production of maple syrup. In late February or early March, my uncles would tap the maple trees in the sugar bush at the northeast corner of the farm. Because power augurs, vacuum pumps, and plastic pipe and bags were yet to come, they would drill tap holes by hand with a brace and bit, then hammer in a galvanized iron spout from which a tin bucket was suspended (galvanized buckets were being introduced) and through which the sap would run. Too many holes would draw off too much sap and harm the tree. The usual number was one to four, but the big grandmother tree, as it was called, could take eight.

For the trees to run well, temperatures at night had to fall below freezing and rise in the day; 50 to 55 degrees Fahrenheit was desirable. Without this alternation, the sap did not run and a prolonged warm spell would eventually spoil its quality. When the sap was running, the men would collect it every day, dumping the buckets into a large galvanized-iron gathering tank on a sled drawn by horses, and then, at the sugarhouse, into a wooden storage tank (lined with galvanized iron) from which it could be admitted as needed into the evaporator, or boiling pan.

Probably built in the 1880s, the sugarhouse was a rough, wood-frame building, approximately fifteen by twenty-five feet, plus a woodshed, supported by loose stone piers and covered with a tar-paper roof. The floor was dirt except for a cement pad on which one stood while drawing off the syrup and which supported the arch, or steel frame, and firebox under the evaporator. The sugarhouse sheltered the heart of the operation, the most critical step of the sugar maker's art: the boiling of the thin, watery sap to produce syrup of the desired sweetness and required weight. Vermont law said that a gallon of syrup had to weigh eleven pounds; the more it was boiled, the higher the sugar content and the greater the weight. In those days there was no other grading system or legal requirement. Now syrup is graded by color, the light amber product having the most delicate flavor and commanding the highest price. Darker grades have a stronger flavor, which some people prefer for cooking.

Almost anyone who was strong enough could collect sap, but only an experienced and knowledgeable sugar maker like Uncle

Sherwin could run the evaporator and produce good syrup. The pan was about twelve feet long and three feet wide, and it rested on a cast-iron base and firebox about waist high. Sap flowed by gravity through a valved pipe from the holding tank and moved slowly back and forth through a series of compartments, the first group called the boiling pan, the next the syrup pan, growing hotter and denser as it traveled. Hanging over it on a string was a piece of salt pork. If the syrup began to boil over, it would hit the salt pork and subside. Some farmers would toss in a dash of cream, which had the same effect. There were stories that the salt-pork method should be kept secret; otherwise, Jewish customers might not buy.

It took 45 to 55 gallons of sap, depending on sugar content, to produce one gallon of syrup, and the rest formed great clouds of sweet-smelling steam, the first thing one noticed on entering the sugarhouse. Most of the vapor was confined by a large hood over the pan and made its way outdoors through the roof vents.

At a critical point, after the boiling liquid reached the far side of the pan, it achieved its proper density and was ready to be drawn off. Today Uncle Sherwin and Larry use a thermometer and a hydrometer (measuring density) to tell when the syrup is ready. In those days Uncle Sherwin poured some syrup from a dipper; if it would "leather-apron"—that is, spread in a broad sheet as it was poured—it was done. The syrup flowed from a valve through a thick felt filter into a clean pail. From there it was almost immediately put up in cans, mainly gallons and a few half-gallons, but not the smaller sizes found today. A stick-on label bore the Lester name.

Since it takes enormous energy to evaporate such great quantities of water, sugar making depended on a large supply of wood. The wood produced great heat, and the operator had to be sure to keep enough sap in the evaporator so as not to damage the pan by overheating. When the boiling became less vigorous, Uncle Sherwin would open the big iron doors at one end of the firebox with a wood poker (he did not want his face that close to the intense fire inside), quickly poke the fire, throw in more wood, and close the doors. At any time during boiling but most voluminously during reloading, thousands of sparks would follow the draft up the tall smokestack, and at night they could be seen from afar, streaming away on the wind until they burned themselves out in the blackness.

Sugaring was hard work, but the family loved it. It usually lasted until early April and it had its own demands, skills, rhythm, and ceremonies, uniting pleasure and labor. Sometimes the boiling went late into the night and occasionally Uncle Sherwin and Aunt Ellrena would pack a lunch and go to the sugarhouse together. Everyone liked the syrup, the soothing sound of it bubbling in the pan, the nose-tingling fragrance rising in the clouds of steam, the intense sweetness hot from the evaporator with a fresh, dunked doughnut chased by sour pickles, the rich golden-amber color pouring from the valve into the strainer or held up in a jar against the light, and even the surprising heft of it in the shiny tin cans, signifying work well done and money to come. Family and friends from the city would come to the sugarhouse, sit on a bench in the steam, and receive the customary cup and doughnuts and pickles. There was time to talk and the talk almost always was about the run, the weather, the quality of the sap. It was like hunters talking about hunting, as if by unspoken agreement the rest of life was suspended for a while. So they did not talk about illness, death, the war, or the farms that were going under.

Finally, there was the sense that although the calendar may not have announced the new season, the maple trees had. Man was capturing and distilling to its essence the very lifeblood of the tree. The buds, which had formed the previous year, were about to swell with enfolded leaf, while within the dark, skeletal form nutrients were making their way up from the dead ground to the very extremities of the spreading branches. Only the surface of things was dead and frozen, a condition of arrested animation about to be softened and enlivened by the sun and the mysterious powers within, just as fields and lanes and roads were about to turn to mud, one of Vermont's most conspicuous signs of spring. Poets have seen the branching of life itself in the veins of rivulets in sand and mud. The Vermonter might think first of old jokes about mud season — yes, said the man whose hat was seen moving across the surface of the mud, I will be all right as long as I have my horse under me — and if he has ever traveled farther south, even in Connecticut or New Jersey, he will know that spring in Vermont is a starved season, its splendor distinctly muted. It is a time of promise, but of a promise made in a whisper.

Spring was also the time to mend fences, pick stones, and whitewash the interior of the stable. The men pulled the recalcitrant barbed wire tight from post to post with a so-called fence-fixing tool and stapled it in place. If a post had to be replaced, one man held the sharpened piece of cedar or locust, the native species most resistant to rot, while another man drove it in with a heavy maul. Even in this simple task, there was a right and a wrong way. The right way was to hold the post and avert one's eyes, for it took an unusually steady man to watch the maul descend without flinching.

Most of the pastures and fields were bounded by wire fencing — split rails had long gone — but a few were marked by stone walls, started at the very beginning of the farm, repaired in the spring, and added to with the stones that appeared as if by magic from the bowels of the earth. It was a common joke all over New England that a field's best crop was stones, and, indeed, there was a piece of equipment designed for harvesting them.

Picking stones, as the job was called, meant lifting or rolling them
onto a stone boat, a flat sledge with a turned-up front or nose,
and drawing them by horse to the nearest wall. It was heavy
work.

Each spring my uncles bought quicklime, mixed it with water
in a barrel, and sprayed it on the walls and ceiling of the stable
with a pump. There were traveling whitewashers who would do
it for them, but they often covered the windows as well. When
quicklime and water is first mixed, the solution gets very hot, and
in the old days people made fish bombs by corking the solution
quickly in a bottle and throwing it into a stream, where it would
explode, stunning the fish.

It was not for some years that I came to understand the
annual cycle of work on the farm. That the summer had a form
I discerned even as a child, and still more obvious to me was the
pattern of the day. Uncle Sherwin got up at four o'clock. After
a piece of toast and, in midsummer, some salt and water, he would
start morning chores. In the winter the cows would be in the barn
overnight, but in summer they were in pasture, and while they
knew it was milking time and would be moving toward the barn,
sometimes they had to be herded under the bridge and back up
the lane. In the barn they stepped over the gutter and stuck their
heads through the stanchions. A stanchion consisted of two vertical iron rails with wood facing, about five feet tall, attached top
and bottom to a rugged frame. One of the rails was movable and
could be opened wide to receive the cow's head and closed part
way to hold it in place. The cows faced the center of the stable,
an aisle called the feed alley, from which Uncle Sherwin could
put hay, grain, and ensilage into the manger, the space just in
front of the cows. Between every two cows was a metal watering
bowl piped to the barn's water supply. When a cow's muzzle
depressed a lever at the bottom of the bowl, a valve opened to

let in water. Behind the cows was the manure gutter and beyond the gutter, by the outside wall of the stable, a walkway in which the men could work.

The cows fed while they were being milked, so in the winter Uncle Sherwin would first bring ensilage from the silo in the two-wheeled cart and shovel some in front of each cow. The full cart, very heavy, had to be guided down a ramp to the stable, and I admired the skill with which he turned the cart on the incline by grabbing one rapidly moving wheel. Next came the grain, brought from the Eastern States Farmers Exchange warehouse in 100-pound burlap bags and dumped into a wooden barrel which he tilted and rolled as he scooped out each cow's portion. The cart and the barrel each had its distinctive, rhythmic rumble, as much a part of chores to me as the milking itself. In the summer the cows usually got plenty of grass, but in the cold months, or if the pasture was low, Uncle Sherwin would fork hay down from the loft overhead or drag it by the forkful from the mows of the attached big barn and put it in front of the cows. If a cow had mastitis, an infection of the udder, he would administer sulfanil-amide pills, giant capsules pushed down the throat with a balling gun or dissolved in a bottle of water and poured down.

An electric vacuum pump, rhythmically throbbing, powered the milking system, producing the vacuum in the pipes, pail, and teat cups that sucked the milk from the cow's bag. In 1944 the Empire milking system was in use. The machine sat on the floor and, with its two sets of cups, would milk two cows at once. After the 1947 flood, when the farm installed the new Surge system, a single machine was suspended under the cow from a leather strap over her back. After wiping the bag with a wet rag, Uncle Sherwin would strip off some milk, that is, produce a few squirts from each teat by hand to see if it was good and to give a boost to those cows that would let down their milk more easily for the machine if first stripped by hand. He would then attach the suction cups and move on to the next cow. For the thirty to forty cows, he used two double machines, one pail for two cows. Despite the efficiency of mechanization, he believed that if a farmer had enough help, he would do better to milk by hand. There would be fewer problems with mastitis, a disease which produced garget — unsalable, ropy, off-colored milk. At the Stockbridge School of Agriculture, where Uncle Sherwin studied, the cows were milked by hand.

Some were easy milkers, some were hard, but when a cow was finished, on the average in five minutes, the milk was emptied into a pail and the hired man would take it to the creamery at the end of the barn and pour it into a forty-quart can, the kind people now buy at yard sales. When the can was full, he would put it in the cooler.

There were other chores to do while the cows were being milked. Somebody had to feed the bull, which received the same diet as the cows. Small compared to a big Holstein bull today, Johnny was a good-sized Jersey at 1,600 to 1,800 pounds, and he was to me a massive beast indeed. I stayed well back from the great swinging head which came thrusting out of the pen to reach the food. The weaned calves had to eat too, first a mixture of milk and water off a man's fingers, then out of a pail, and eventually grain and hay. The entire barn floor was made of concrete, but a bed of sawdust was kept under the cows, and, as needed, someone would hoe splattered manure or wet sawdust into the gutter and pull clean sawdust into place.

When all the cows were milked and fed, they were turned back to pasture, except in cold weather, when they were let into the enclosed barnyard for fresh air and exercise before being returned to the barn. After a breakfast of oatmeal, soft-boiled eggs, home fries, toast, and milk, men continued the day's work.

One of my uncles would take the milk to the city, to the dairy (usually called a creamery), which resold it locally. From the dairy he would go to the hospital to pick up the two or three barrels of garbage for the pigs. In exchange for the garbage, twice a week he would take trash from the hospital to the city dump — in the days before sanitary landfills a much more exciting place, where I could see rats and find discarded treasures. Sometimes my uncle needed other things in the city, a part for a machine, grain for the animals, something for the house.

The work for the rest of the day until evening chores (the second milking) depended on the season, but a number of special jobs stand out in my mind. Twice a day Uncle Milo put down water for the hens and scooped grain pellets from a bin to pour into long wooden feeders on the henhouse floor. The hens ran free in the henhouse and enclosed yard and they laid their eggs in raised nests (wooden boxes); the elevation pleased the hens and kept the nests cleaner. Some hens did not want to give up their eggs. Their peck could draw blood, so the egg gatherer learned to grab the hen's neck before retrieving the egg. After a year the hens were beheaded, plucked, gutted, and transformed into roasts, stews, or chicken pie.

To feed the pigs, Uncle Sherwin shoveled garbage into a trough directly from the barrels. There were usually thirty to fifty pigs, perhaps as many as seventy when litters were born, and they received little grain because the garbage, the hospital's uneaten food, was very rich. Later the state decided that garbage had to be boiled before it could be fed, and still later a new hospital was built with disposals, and the good pig feed was no more.

There were two pigpens, one attached to the back of the horse barn, one a lean-to on the old corn barn. Uncle Sherwin slaughtered in the corn barn, but after it went down in the flood, he built a new pig barn with an attached slaughterhouse. He shoveled out the pens three to four times a year, and although it wasn't considered a terrible job, he still has unpleasant dreams of standing up to his knees in pig manure. Richer in nitrogen than cow manure, it made excellent fertilizer.

The farm kept five or six breeding sows, which produced litters of eight to ten young spring and fall. Unless he was kept for breeding, a male pig was castrated before he was a month old, since castrated pigs grew faster and were less subject to rages. A seated helper would hold the squealing pig upside down on his lap, spreading the hind legs. Uncle Sherwin would squeeze the scrotum, make one incision on each side to release the testicles and one slice to cut them off, then wash the wounds with alcohol. It took no more than a minute.

Weighing up to 300 pounds, boars were, like bulls, dangerous and unpredictable, even more dangerous, some said, because almost impossible for an unarmed man to subdue by pain except by a blow on the snout — and the snout is very close to jaws so powerful they can crush a man's leg or arm in a single bite. Faced with an angry bull, a man may be able to grab the nose ring and control him. Some say that a particularly lucky and agile man might be able to control a bull by seizing his testicles, but on the farm they believed that one should work the other end.

Castration was understood as part of a more comprehensive, if vaguely articulated, notion about untamed sexuality and destructiveness. Sexuality for man or beast was never discussed as a right or as an expressive, fulfilling act or, except as an occasional joke in the field, as a pleasure desirable simply in and of itself. While not insisting that sex existed only for the sake of reproduction, the family probably believed that that was its highest justification, and they certainly believed that it was a dangerous, unsettling force in both man and animal. It was tamed between men and women by marriage and by habits of courtesy and mutual deference. If irregular liaisons existed in the neighborhood, they were never mentioned in my hearing, although some years after my first summer on the farm, I did hear of a woman of easy virtue, as she was called, who had moved into an old schoolhouse, now converted to a dwelling. One night a local hired man was said to have knocked on the door and asked for a lesson. Eyeing him critically, the woman said that school was not in session.

Slaughtering was a regular part of farm life. As mentioned earlier, Uncle Sherwin killed cows on the big barn floor with hammer and knife as his uncle and grandfather had done before him. He shot pigs in the head with a .22, aiming at the spot where a horizontal line between the ears and a vertical line between the eyes would cross; there was the brain. Once, years later, when I worked on the farm, he gave me the rifle, but my aim was poor and the wounded pig ran in a frenzy all over the slaughterhouse until Uncle Sherwin brought it down with a second shot. He then bled the pig, hoisted him by the hamstrings, and dipped him in boiling water to loosen the bristles. He removed the bristles with a circular hog scraper, also known as a candlestick, which in the old days was actually used to hold a candle. Gutted, beheaded, and sawed in two lengthwise, the carcass, now two sides of pork, was sold to local merchants. The heart, liver, and tongue were also sold, the guts were thrown in the field, the blood ran into a drain, and, if someone felt enterprising, the bladder could be inflated, dried, and tossed like a football.

There were duties at the other end of life as well. Cows could calve on their own, but it was prudent to keep an eye on them in case they needed help. Uncle Sherwin knew how to straighten out the calf if it was coming crooked; with special chains and a handle, he would turn the calf so that the two front legs, with head lying on top, would come first. Occasionally he needed a vet. In cold weather cows calved in the barn, but the pasture was cleaner. Often the dog played a part, too; he would pull out the afterbirth and eat it.

There were always repairs, maintenance, and medical care of the animals. Uncle Sherwin was something of a veterinarian, dehorning and vaccinating as well as castrating and attending at births. Once, when a sow stepped on a piglet, cutting open its abdomen, he cleaned the protruding innards, stuffed them back inside, and sewed up the gash; the patient lived. Farm life intensifies the condition of the village or city householder, for whom weekends are times of repair and maintenance. Add to the demands of one's body, automobile, house, and lawn those of seventy-five to eighty cows and calves, thirty to fifty pigs, one hundred hens, three horses, two trucks, one tractor, one car, various other large machines, several barns and sheds, vast lengths of walls and fences, many gates, a large accumulation of tools from more than one generation, and, of course, the land itself — add all these and it seems clear that the various arts of farming will not suffice without an overarching habit of attention.

Looking back at the lifetime of attention required of Uncle Sherwin and Uncle Milo, I see in it both a reminder and a warning. In some significant if not ultimate sense, we become what we do whether our real doing is work or pleasure. In some instances the shaping is most obviously seen in our bodies — the dancer's lithe and limber frame, the office worker's soft roundness, Uncle Sherwin's solid muscularity. But more significantly, our native powers are challenged, formed, and limited by the tasks we set them, and our hearts and minds are filled with the smells and colors, the hopes and fears, of what we do. I saw a sign in the window of a styling salon, touting the dedication of the stylist: HAIR IS ALWAYS ON HIS MIND. With rare exceptions, no good work is done independent of such absorption and self-shaping.

Probably no farm boy of seven or eight ever thought of the

work of the day and year as cycles or, perhaps, even of work as an activity distinct from the rest of life. I felt, as a boy, that the work of my uncles was a natural part of life because in fact it happened every day without fuss or commotion, but coming as I did from a village, it was new to me and worthy of comment. My diary reveals this dual aspect.

The thirty-five work entries divide as follows. In five of them, I describe myself as simply going along. In eight, I refer to the men as working alone, suggesting that I either was a bystander or heard about the work at the end of the day. In fourteen, I refer to myself in the first person as working, but in six of the fourteen the men or women are also mentioned as working. And in eight of the entries, I identify with the men as fellow workers and speak in the first-person plural.

In those entries in which I just went along, I accompanied one of my uncles to the summer pasture, probably to check on the cows, or to the hospital "after the garbage" for the pigs, or to another farm "after two hogs," or "up in the corn" with Uncle Milo and the hired man, or "down with the milk" to the creamery, or to the sawmill "after some boards." They were little pleasure trips for me, but in fact I was with the men as they worked and I was gaining a sense of what work meant. It meant, in part, going places, taking things, getting things, checking things. It developed a sense of place, of different places: the farm as center with its own character and way of being, the place that really mattered, and then the other places, the lesser places, where from time to time one had to go — the hospital, the dump, the creamery, the grain warehouse, another farm.

Sometimes I am an observer or a listener, reporting what I have seen and heard. I note when "the men went up and fixed the fence and mowed thistles," when "the men started cutting hay in bridge meadow" to the west of the road, when "they vaccinated the little pigs," when "the mechanic came up and fixed the hay truck," and when "the men put up the hay machines" at the end of the season. I follow the progress of haying over the weeks and remark that the men "got in eight loads" or "drew in twelve loads," and of this last I say, "Today has been a very good hay day."

The largest category of work entries presents me as a worker, with or without mention of others. On the fourth, fifth, and sixth days of my visit, I was given the task of sprouting potatoes, that is, breaking off the shoots growing on what remained of last year's crop in the dim light of the potato bin in the cellar. If not broken off, the shoots would consume the potato, shriveling it until it could not be eaten. "I started sproutind potatoes today," and, then, on the next two days, "I am still sprouting my potatoes" and "finished potatoes today." Apparently the job seemed long on the second day — I was "still" at it — but I identified with it, for they were "my" potatoes. I can still remember the cool, damp air, the faint light from the cellar window, and the roughness of the potato skins against my hands. One other job appears to have become mine alone, although in retrospect it seems unlikely: "I have started to feed the hens today."

Whether I noticed a difference between the jobs I truly performed and those in which I was merely allowed to feel useful, I cannot say, and perhaps in the larger scheme of things it did not matter: "I helped . . . fix the truck today," and "I milked two cows tonight one was pretty steppy," "I drove the horses," "I drove the hay truck." By small increments, pretending shades into reality; holding the reins becomes truly driving. For better or worse, there was no rite of passage, just an accumulation of experience and knowledge so that one day, had I stayed on the farm, I would by imperceptible degrees have become a man and a farmer.

Among the adventures of my life that might in these informal times count as rites of passage — the trip to Europe, a summer on a salmon boat in Alaska, the discovery of a wider world in college, the entry into a deeper world of thought years later, the mysteries of eros — one did occur on the farm, but in one of those later summers when I returned to work. For two days, while Uncle Sherwin and Aunt Ellrena took a rare vacation, I was left in charge of the farm, the chief responsibility of which was milking the cows — all of them — correctly. I broke an upraised cutter bar when I drove the tractor under a low branch, but I took it to the blacksmith and had it repaired. Otherwise the days passed without incident, and I felt I had earned my keep and was ready for what lay ahead.

In other entries I explicitly refer to myself as working along with the men and women. "I helped . . . pick peas but I ate more than I picked. I shucked them for Grandma." Some of this work, like the chores above, was actually useful, such as signaling to the men when the forkload of hay had reached the loft: "The men started puting hay in the horse barn and I called off for the men," and "I called off for the men west of the big barn and the sun was hot." On other occasions, my help must have been marginal at best: "The men built a fence around the meadow and I help them," or "I helped get the miserable old cattle back in where they belong. We fixed the fence."

With one questionable exception, taking wood to the hired man's house, it is on the twenty-ninth day of the visit that I first use "we" to describe my participation in the work of the farm. (There are seven other work entries in which I do not distinguish between my contribution and that of others, and two entries in which I use both the singular and the plural pronoun.) "Today was the 'miserablest' hay-day we had so far," "We drew in ten loads of hay today," and "We had a thunder showee but we were lucky for we only had a small load out." When all the crop was in, I simply note, "We finished haying today." In one entry, I apparently felt part of a 4-H meeting as well as of the day's work: "We had a 4H meeting today. We went . . . after a cow. She was going to have a calf but she had all ready had her calf. We did not get there soon enough."

In short, a child learned early to identify with the men, women, and work of the farm. The farm family did not confuse childhood with adulthood, the labor was not harsh or exploitative, there were games, toys, and plenty of what today we call recreation; but it was not, for all that, a child-centered environment. A generation later the state of Vermont was to adopt "child-centered education" as its official policy, and every school district was put to work identifying how the unique needs of every child could be met. It was seductive rhetoric and seemed so obviously aimed at the good of the child that to oppose it was to expose one's heart as very black and one's neck as very red.

On the farm, no sharp distinction was made between the needs of the child and those of the grown-ups. Children were obviously on their way to becoming grown-ups, and if the family had been pressed to think about it in these terms, it would probably have said that the purpose or end of childhood — and therefore of child-rearing and education — was to move children to adulthood as fast as possible. And while it was certainly recognized that not all farm children would grow up to be farmers, the adults on this farm, at least, believed that they enjoyed not just a way of making a living but a way of life, and they had enough self-confidence to think that if they could raise succeeding generations to be like themselves, they would be doing a fine and worthy thing. There are questions they may not have asked — I never heard them asked — such as how effective were their means, how comprehensive their conception of adulthood, and how relevant their vision of the future to what fate held in store. But whatever questions they did not ask, they resisted longer than most the modern tendency to divide childhood and adulthood, work and play, workplace and home.

I understood my uncles' work better at seven than many people do their fathers' work at twenty-one. But what did it mean to "understand" it? First of all, of course, the work was physically present to be seen — it was daily action performed before my very eyes — and some of its materials could be touched, heard, smelled, and tasted as well. From hours with the cows at milking time, I still carry on the palms of my hands the silky blood-warmth of their flanks, in my ears their slow munching, in my nose their animal sweetness, on my tongue the too-warm richness of their milk. Work was immersion, understandable as water is when you swim in it.

It was also rational. I could see and grasp the connections of things. The planting, which I knew had taken place, and the ripening, mowing, drying, and storing, which I saw, were not random phenomena but related parts of a comprehensible whole, which, in fact, did not stop there but included feeding the cows to produce milk which could be drunk and sold. Selling brought money and money I already understood, as the diary shows.

There were books, trips to Rutland, an occasional movie (I wept for the sufferings of Lassie at war and learned to hate the Germans), but most of my sense of the world that summer came to me from the calm and loving order of the household and the daily challenges of field and barn. Life was immediate, earnest, difficult, but neither baffling nor overpowering — men and women were equal to the task — and I am sure that it is in part to this picture of daily victories that I owe my sense of ease in the world. I am comfortable on the street, at the podium, in smoky rooms, at the office, wherever men and women congregate, work, negotiate, debate the affairs of the town. It is not a matter of grand successes, but of feeling confident and at home. Lucky in my circumstances, shielded by accident from many of the calamities of mankind, I know that the world is a precarious place and that my life is a sheltered nook in the rush of history. I know it, but I do not feel it in my bones, and so, like most blessings, my confidence is a mixed one. It is harder for me than for some to grasp the horror of things.

Work, then, was not only a process and a result, it was an engagement of the entire being and thus accessible, in part, to the child. In what proportions the various faculties were engaged and what it did to them over time, I could only dimly see. That it strengthened bodies was apparent to me. So, too, were its claims on patience, perseverance, prudence, and courage. A fence could be mended fast or slowly, potatoes could be dusted lazily or briskly, but Uncle Sherwin could not speed up the vacuum pump and suck cows dry in a minute nor could he whip the ground to make the corn grow. Having done what man could do, there was nothing left but to wait. And as in most work that does not spring from sudden insight (and even insight requires preparation), the only way to get from beginning to end was to lift one more stone, then one more stone, or to haul load after load, one the same as the other, until all was done. And within the realm left to man and not in the hands of the gods, prudence and courage were all in all. Prudence required knowledge, indeed was a kind of knowledge, the ability to calculate the likely effect of things, of the cards dealt by chance and of the measures to be taken by man. Some of it came from a blend of inherited practice and up-to-date technical advice: the kind and quantity of fertilizer for this soil and climate, the best seed mix for hay, the right moisture content for corn. Some of it was a kind of sixth sense, a knack outside the realm of art, strictly understood, some unteachable sense of what would work and what would not — a feel for the swing of a maul or a tractor's speed, an eye for the balance of a load of hay or an animal's health, an ear for the timing of an engine or a gear's pull. And courage was the ability to exercise and enliven the other virtues despite temptations to the contrary. It made patience a hopeful thing, not mere resignation, and gave spirit to perseverance, saving it from brute plodding. Courage required memory of what happened when one did not exercise the other virtues; it was, therefore, a kind of applied prudence.

As I grew to manhood and came to know something of specialization — the knowledge and dexterity of the surgeon, the limitations of the assembly worker — I saw the necessary diversity of a farmer's skills in a different light. My uncles were, in a partial way, mechanics, carpenters, plumbers, electricians, butchers, veterinarians, agronomists, geneticists. Farmers and small-town dwellers praised the resourcefulness of the jack-of-all-trades, and if they completed the saying — and master of none — it was with humorous self-deprecation, not true regret. Some of this my father, himself a farm boy, passed on, and even now I can repair a toilet, build a set of steps, glaze a window, set a lock. If I had to, I could probably support myself as a handyman, although the pride I once took in my versatility has long since been tinged with doubt, for every nail driven is a sentence unread or unwritten.

What raises the farmer above the handyman is his grasp of the entire enterprise. The question for the farm is not what else the farmer might do if he did not repair the truck himself, but what relation that repair has to farming and to ends beyond. For to farm is to repair trucks and fertilize the soil and practice the rudiments of a dozen other specialties. Farming is precisely all of these things bent to a single end, and the real question is of the nature and quality of the end. Farming is the master art, the understanding and management of a comprehensive enterprise that makes sense of every constituent part and without which, no matter how proficient, no individual skill achieves its full meaning. The meaning of an art includes the end it serves, and no more significant question can be asked of the practitioner than to what end he labors. But what of farming itself? Is it embraced by a still more comprehensive art? The echoes of Grandmother's answer grow faint.

Returning to the more familiar aspects of work, again I find the concrete and abstract interfused. By turns bloody, dirty, dangerous, strenuous, relaxed, deadening, and enlivening, farm work links the grittiest, most immediate encounters with the natural world to unpredictable, impersonal forces that move like the whims of a god.

Those whose relations to meat begin with plastic-wrapped ground round and end with hamburger on a bun may have trouble imagining some of the details of Uncle Sherwin's work: the complex, sensuous immediacy of a hammer blow to the head, the grunt of massive brain damage, the gurgle and brightness of blood from the jugular, the spasms of dying nerves, the smell and color of spilled guts. And all that was only a stage that began with a calf's birth in a field or stable, struggling to stand on uncertain legs, eating, growing, feeling the sun and rain and the warm shoulders of others of its kind, hearing human voices. Uncle Sherwin lived through the cycles of things, not only the daily round and the curve of the seasons but conception, growth, and death, and part of the cycle was blood and part was dirt. Something deep in man despises or fears contact with that which is cast off, and however much we tell ourselves that manure is no less natural than the grain from which it comes, we cannot overcome our aversion to it. "Shit" is a dirty word for good reason. It is the farmer's lot to deal with it. It is truly part of a cycle since it is fertilizer to help produce more grain, but it is the part most of us can avoid thinking about. Oddly enough, as our domestic arrangements become ever more splendid and sanitized—our bathrooms little palaces of gleaming tile, ornamental soaps, fluffy white towels, and odor-venting toilets—our language becomes more scatological, and even young women, to say nothing of the men, now have on their lips what my uncles had on a shovel.

Dangerous, strenuous, relaxed . . . Farming is still one of the most dangerous occupations. The physical engagement with animals, machines, and the treacherous surface of the earth is so intimate and continuous that accidents do happen. Even as I write, I can think of a farmer-cousin whose badly injured back, in a brace, will keep him off the tractor for months, another cousin whose hand was mangled only months ago in a barn cleaner, and an uncle who lost a thumb to some machine or other. With the advantages of artificial insemination, fewer farms keep bulls now, but a generation or two ago every farm had stories of injuries or near escapes from the sudden anger of a bull, and now and then a grim pig story, too, like the one not far from my boyhood home in which a boar caught and ate a child. Some stories have the makings of folklore. I knew a farmer whose wife helped with the barn chores. Having warned her repeatedly about the bull, he was alarmed when he heard a terrible bellowing from the barnyard. As he told it, first he was afraid the bull was killing his wife, but when he rounded the corner of the barn, he was afraid the wife was killing his bull. Attacked, she had defended herself with a crowbar, and the bull was now on its knees, roaring in pain and terror, blood pouring from both nostrils. Even cats and chickens could be dangerous, as a friend of my father once reported. Asked about his bandaged hand, the man replied that he always killed a chicken for Sunday dinner, and the cat always ran off with the head. This time his aim was bad and he took off his thumb instead. He reached for it, thinking to ice it and rush to the hospital, but the cat was quicker and he never saw it again.

At the peak of activity, farm work is strenuous indeed, not so much the force required for any given act as the repeated demand for energy. One forkful of hay in a dusty, hot loft almost anyone can handle. To be still at it three hours later requires stamina. By the law of contrasts, however, the relaxation between loads, the complete cessation of effort, is as pleasant to the farmer as the hour after a long run to the runner. Those whose bodies are never pushed never know the sweetness of rest. There are other pleasures. In my memory the most welcome drink was switchel, a concoction of vinegar, maple syrup, ginger, and water, made by Aunt Ellrena or Grandmother and brought in a tin lard bucket to the men in the hayfield on hot summer days. Other tasks, requiring less effort, soothed through rhythmic repetition: the wheel and engine vibrations of a tractor, the gait of a team of horses, the sounds and motions of milking.

Farming not only requires strength, it develops it. For the founder, the effect on the body was one of the principal benefits of agriculture, the work "most conducive to health, long life, and happiness. It gives a healthy tone and action to the lungs, the heart expands and beats freely, the blood vessels perform their natural duties, the bone cords and muscles by being constantly in use become developed and strengthened, and these, supported by a due proportion of flesh and fat, makes man in reality the lord of creation." Without moderation, work itself becomes destructive, however. The founder preached temperance in all things but could not always practice it, and, as Grandmother recalled, it was his anger with the lazy men and his furious overexertion when he showed them how to work that led to his death.

Farm work is both deadening and enlivening. I suspect that our sense of ourselves, moment by moment, has more to do with our happiness than we care to admit. For some the vision of final ends and vast purposes is steady enough to keep their spirits bubbling through all the vicissitudes of the day. More common are the grimmer heroes whose memory of high intention enables them to persevere even when the taste of goodness has left the tongue.

It isn't so clear what raises or lowers the spiritual temperature when ultimate purpose fades. No doubt it is partly a gift of nature, a happy blend that gives to some people their peculiar buoyancy, but just as our minds are filled with, and therefore characterized by, what we attend to, so too our hearts beat to the rhythms of work and play. As in so much else, farm work aims at a middle state, neither the suppression of the animal spirits nor their exhilarating release. At its best, it encourages an energetic sobriety, neither the dullness of the slave mines nor the exuberance of plunder. It is one glass of wine.

This is the personal dimension, the mix of infighting and dance that characterizes the work of a farm. But far over it all, yet touching it vitally, are the vast natural patterns of weather, climate, and disease. Two weeks before these words were written, an apple orchard not five miles from my home was struck by a hailstorm, wiping out a crop worth a million dollars. Far more surprising than the antique rites of propitiation and gratitude, the fat and grain on the sacrificial fire, is the absence of such rites in our contemporary world. Accepting on faith a vision from those who say they know, we have driven the gods from the temples. We are left with what we call nature, but we often mean the inexplicable, chance.

For Grandmother and my uncles, there was an imagined coexistence of the hand of God and the workings of a nature that was midway between divinity and the operations of mechanical laws. They would have been uncomfortable if pressed to describe the relationship between the two or to declare whether they believed there was none. When weather or disease caused damage, it was nature, not God, that was named, but nature was not simply a malevolent force. While they had to fight her as she sought to dissolve the artful bonds which held things in useful forms, they also felt they were cooperating with her as they made use of her powers of renewal and growth. They would have listened without objection to the phrase "harnessing the power of nature," but it is unlikely that in their hearts they ever thought they could really do it except in a most partial way. Through nature they could accomplish fine things, but that nature herself was ever under their control would have struck them as not quite blasphemous but erroneous and perhaps presumptuous. There was much to remind them that they were not the lords of creation, despite the bold words of the founder. What fell to their hands to do they did with all their strength and craft, but they knew they worked at the center of a mystery, the motions of which they could neither influence nor predict. If they ever prayed for rain or sun, I never heard them. They were not fearful people or angry, and they thought of the ultimate order of things as benevolent if inscrutable. They were confident, but wary.

Their work was conditioned by one other fact, obvious but immensely important. They owned the land. They not only owned it, they were tied to it by generations of memory and experience, by living on it as well as working it, and by the long-range nature of the enterprise in which change was measured in years for crops, in generations for animals, in decades for machines, and in potential centuries for major buildings. The farm still uses a John Deere tractor I drove when I worked there over forty years ago. Ownership of this sort produces a proud and independent spirit, and the humblest tasks are transformed when they are part of something prominent, long-lasting, and dignified. The price, of course, is a loss of individual freedom and the danger, in prolonged bad times, of being dragged down by the failure of the enterprise.

Going out of farming is not as simple as quitting a job, and while many have negotiated it successfully, there are others who have been ground down over the years by worsening conditions that sap the spirit as well as the bank account. And in an age of great geographic and social mobility, even the successful ones may feel the constraints of work which holds them to one piece of ground, often under the eye of their elders, in an undertaking of indefinite duration.

"The subtlety of the serpent and the beauty of the fruit" were too much for mother Eve, the founder said, and for their transgression our first parents lost paradise. It was by the sweat of the brow that Uncle Milo and Uncle Sherwin raised their crops and fed their animals. If this were all, life would have been grim, but as it was, work was the honorable struggle that brought together heart and hand, memory and hope, nature and art.

V · *Animals and Other Living Things*

. . . we see that the supreme being made the earth for the use of man: the beast, the bird, and fishes, the root herb and flowers, the cereal grains and the fruit-bearing trees.

HENRY LESTER, *Man Made for Agriculture*

The early training of the horse has much to do [to] make his future character and usefulness. His disposition will assimilate to that of his breaker.

HENRY LESTER, *On Horses and Horsemen*

Of the time when she [the founder's wife] lived on Lester Meadows in Chittenden, and hearing the frightening call of the panthers, sounding like babies crying in the woods. Bears, too, were very plentiful, seeing them very often when they went for the cows, and one as bold as to visit the pigpen and carry one home for its supper.

PAULINE WILLIAMS, *As I Remember*

☙❧

I shot two sparrows with my bb-gun. they are the hardest little pest to get a shot at.

I milked two cows tonight one was pretty steppy.

The cows got out and ran for the hay meadow, they came like stampede through the gate.

Robert Muggsy and I got a wood chuck today and we skinned him.

CHARLES FISH, *Diary Book*

☙❧

In my brief record of that summer there are about fifty references to animals, guns, bow and arrows, a hunting knife, hunting, and fishing. Of them, seven are to the BB gun, ten to woodchucks, ten to fishing, and seventeen to domestic animals including cows, horses, a pony, pigs, hens, rabbits, and dogs. And there are, of course, many references to people, from Grandmother to the homicidal maniac.

Add the remarks on hay, potatoes, and the vegetable garden, and it becomes apparent that my day reflected, in boyish proportions, the farm's engagement with living things. In large measure, the art of farming was an art of the use of living things, including people. With few exceptions, this use interrupted the life cycle at a critically important time, for only wild things (and not all of them), human beings, and sometimes pets were allowed to die without regard to utility. Everything else was harvested in keeping with the biblical teaching noted in the founder's essay: "He next created man in his own image, male and female created he them, and gave them dominion over the earth, the sea, the fishes, the beasts, the birds, the herb-yielding seed, and the fruit-bearing tree. He created all things for man." Bull calves went immediately to the cattle dealer to end up as veal; unproductive cows and hens were slaughtered; it was said that pigs should not see their six-month birthday (in fact they were killed between six and ten months at two hundred pounds); hay, corn, and vegetables were gathered at their nutritional peak; and when a maple tree began to die, perhaps after three hundred years, it was cut for firewood.

It is apparent to me now that the life cycle which figures so largely in my memory of farm work was not a wholly natural phenomenon any more than is marriage or the pursuit of money or the death of a warrior before the gates of his city; for while the basic life stuff, the genetic potential, was a gift of nature, everything else owed its character to man's calculating mind. And even the genetic package was touched by artful manipulation, for where a thousand years ago was the Holstein cow, the Hampshire hog, the Rhode Island Red chicken? Like English bulldogs, French poodles, Irish wolfhounds, and Labrador retrievers, the animals of the farm took the impress of their master's hand, so that their "nature" and their "natural" environment are inextricable from the breeding pens of some North Sea herdsman or the laboratory of a university geneticist.

My very notion of nature now unsettled, I look in one direction at the grasses of the field, green in the summer sun, and see behind them in shadowy form pencil and paper, carefully labeled packets of seed, neatly marked experimental plots; and in the other direction, off the farm into the city and beyond, I see the councils of state and, behind them, the quiet rooms of study where poets and thinkers, our true founders, shape and reshape our moral and political being. Nature is elusive.

In cows my uncles looked for a combination of high milk volume and high butterfat. The farm's annual volume averaged between 8,000 and 10,000 pounds per cow, and the butterfat content averaged about 3.4 percent; the higher the fat, the higher the sale price. My uncles' herd of Jerseys, Holsteins, and milking shorthorns was formed over the years by trial and error. There was no artificial insemination then or at least none that had reached small Vermont farms, so my uncles did not have access to bloodlines from across the country. The hogs were Jersey Durocs, Chester Whites, and Yorkshires. The hens were Hall Cross, sometimes Rhode Island Reds; a good layer would produce about two hundred eggs per year. There were three horses that summer: the big team, Fanny and Dick, and the small driving horse, Kit. There was to be one more team, Chub and Duke, one a Percheron, the other a Clydesdale, that worked until the late 1940s, at the end only for sugaring.

Most of the cows had names or were known by some distinctive mark. A small farm allowed each to have some individuality in the farmer's mind, and my uncles were the kind of herdsmen who recognized that individuality. The cows also needed to be identified for record keeping, so the farm kept daily production records and tested for butterfat once a month, using a hand-turned milk-testing machine which separated butterfat by centrifugal force.

I have seen dairy operations of a much larger and more mechanized order in which the owners never touched a cow and the workers who did were employees in the most modern sense of the term, performing specialized tasks on shifts of fixed hours. In one instance, the cows entered the milking parlor in a neat line and stepped onto a rotating platform. One man hosed them off, another washed the bag, another put on the cups, another took them off. What difference did it make that my uncles had the entire care of the animals, knew them by name or markings, owned them, and made every decision regarding their fate? Was there affection? What were its limits? Is there a natural human propensity to like animals for reasons other than utility? Now and then one heard of cruel farmers and there certainly were rough ones, angry or undisciplined men whose hostility leapt out at their animals and, no doubt, at their families, too. Of that there was not the slightest trace in my uncles; even Uncle Sherwin's biting of the cow, though irritable, was more a corrective than an aimless punishment. They were gentle, affectionate men, and everything I can remember suggests that they felt an affection for the cows and horses beyond what was necessary in working with them day after day. (It may have extended to hens and hogs, too, but, except for the playfulness of chicks and piglets, there is less in feathered and bristled creatures to elicit sentiment.) For all that, I have always remembered a conversation with Uncle Sherwin about the way one should regard farm animals. He said that there was not an animal on the place that did not have its price. This meant, of course, that ultimately the animals were commodities, products not only of the arts of breeding and nurture but of economics as well.

Like most farms this one had pets as well as livestock, and they were of two kinds, outdoor and indoor. In my first summer there, the outdoor pets were the barn cats and Muggsy, the dog; the indoor pets were house cats, although in later years there were indoor dogs as well. The barn cats caught mice and showed up at milking time for a dish of milk. Some were very tame, some suspicious and shy, and they all lived in a kind of borderland between the human and the wild. Sometimes over the generations they developed distinctive traits such as extra toes or special markings.

There was nothing in their environment that, broadly considered, was not also in man's, for it was in the meadows, barns, and sheds that they hunted, bred, and raised their young. Their senses took in human beings, cows, dogs, rats, mice, birds, hay, corn, the structure of barns and all the interior parts and contents, took it in, I surmise, as a felt whole with distinct, animating parts. They were in man's environment, yet it was not the same, for they knew the inside, remote, and lower regions where man seldom or never came, and they perceived from angles and heights unfamiliar to man. The felt quality of the whole must for them have been different, even as the vividly seen or scented mouse energized their system as it did not man's.

Only years later, as a man, could I imagine the complexity of interlocking environments, from that of the bacterium in a cow's stomach to that of Grandmother in the house or of Uncle Sherwin in the barn. As a boy, I moved like the cats through a unified world of boundaries and floating elements, some parts more distinct, more appealing, but all of them to me real and natural. I think of myself sitting on a bag of grain in this ancient cow barn, its creaking, dusty antiquity covering its artifice with the mask of nature — it was as if it had always been there — watching the dust motes dance in the sunbeams which penetrated the dirty window, and with my small, quick hands catching flies as intently as a hunter. I moved unthinkingly in this little world, and my easy, undiscriminating acceptance of all its parts, my naturalization, so to speak, became a habitual part of my sense of belonging, giving me strength and comfort but at the same time obscuring the extent to which the world was man-made. I was at home like a cat, and it now strikes me as odd that the very conditions of a healthy belonging should be obstacles to clarity of thought.

I remember from later years the house cats and dogs trained by Aunt Ellrena to do a surprising variety of tricks, but these animals always seemed to me less essentially of the farm than the barn cats who carried on an unseen life as well as a public one. No cat was of great interest, however, compared to Muggsy the outdoor farm dog, a medium-sized, brown, short-haired, muscular creature, with a broad head, blunt muzzle, powerful jaws, and an absolute passion for killing woodchucks. He took pleasure in eating, in being scratched, in lying in the sun, and in fighting with the dog from the neighboring farm—"Joe Thomas (dog) and Muggsy had a bloody battle today. they nsever seem to be friendly"—but if he had been able to contemplate the fitness of things, he would have said that a wise god had made woodchucks so that he could hunt them and thereby fulfill his nature.

My contemplations did not extend to the fitness of things either, but with no squeamishness or remorse I joined the dog in his depredations. The woodchucks were only one of many wild animals on the farm: bats, snakes, red squirrels, gray squirrels, chipmunks, mink, muskrats, foxes, deer, skunks, raccoons. In the summer pasture in the mountains, there were porcupines, bobcats, and bear. In 1944 the coyote had not reached Vermont and the wild turkey had not been reintroduced. Both are abundant now, and recently a wandering moose plunged through the barbed-wire fence behind the old horse barn. Small birds occasionally fell to the BB gun—"I shot two sparrows with my bb-gun. they are the hardest little pest to get a shot at"—but of more interesting game only the woodchuck was accessible, because of its habit of taking refuge in stone walls if cut off from its secure den in the ground. Unless it found a niche under rocks too heavy to move, the woodchuck could be dug out by a determined boy and dog.

"Muggsy and I cornered a wood chuck in the stone wall. We had a lot of fun trying to get him out." With Uncle Bub's help, I poked the woodchuck out where the dog could get him. "And then O boy! Muggsy did shake hin. I tried to skin but it did not work very good." Sometimes the pursuit was fruitless. "Muggsy and I went wood chuck hunting," reads one entry, and on another occasion, "Muggsy cornered a woodchuck in a rock . . . but we could not get him out." Another time, however, "Muggsy and I caught an other woodchuck today and skinned her." The dog always killed the woodchuck by shaking it.

The killing of animals is a curious business. As I grew up and away from the farm and my rural roots, I sometimes found myself in the company of those for whom hunting was distasteful, even immoral. Their aversion was variously grounded — on a gentleness that did not like to inflict pain, on a sense that life was sacred, on a fear that a taste for hurting animals would lead to a taste for hurting people, on a feeling of social superiority that regarded hunting as primitive or unsophisticated or crudely masculine, on a political judgment that hunters were right-wing regressives. They might concede that in some circumstances the good of the species required management, that is, culling, but they did not believe, with good reason, that the hunter's motives were primarily ecological. I had no persuasive defense of the sport and I seldom tried to explain it from the inside, from the perceptions and passions of the hunter himself. Indeed, my own taste for it waned, but it remained in the blood.

The diary presents hunting in its most elemental form, prior to its utility in providing food, its ecological justification, its contribution to fraternal bonding, or its literary and anthropological portrayal as ritual. This was not game management, although my uncles could defend the killing of woodchucks as the elimination of a pest; it was not the cultivation of friendship as, say, in a deer camp; and it was not a rite of passage — no blood mark on the forehead, no admission to the band of warriors — although it came closest to this last. I did think of myself as a hunter, in a class apart. I read books about Indian hunters and white trappers, I arrived at the farm with gun and bow and arrows, and I imagined myself as a woodsman/hunter/Indian, a superior sort of man, skill-ful and brave. But what the diary gives access to is not simply the reenactment of the deeds of these heroes but the actual pas-sions of a boy as hunter, passions which were already becoming literary and socialized but which in those woodchuck-killing days existed as nearly as possible in their pure, that is, primitive form.

Killing things stirred the blood as nothing else I knew. Much of the discipline of life, as I was already coming to know, was imposed in the interest of good order, for harmony and mutual benefit, and in obedience to parental and divine command. For me, a boy, the aim of hunting was the pleasure of artful killing: the caution, the stalking, the cooperation of boy and dog, the technical challenge of digging out the woodchuck, all culminating in the animal's death. The subsidiary pleasures of showing the prize, taking its pelt as a trophy, or seeing the happiness of the dog made sense only in relation to the pursuit and the kill.

Experienced from within, the pleasure appeared to be an end in itself, as does the pleasure of a lover. That the beauty of the beloved might lead to the contemplation of other forms of beauty, as some have believed, was not a thought I could have entertained; that hunting, with its skills of observation, cunning, deception, and force, might be the paradigm for other forms of pursuit and command was almost as remote from my understanding. The farm did not speak of such things. In both cases the deepening of the experience requires wise and timely teaching, without which love and hunting continue to offer only their primary pleasures to intense natures or some softened version to those made quiet by domesticity or the gentler delights of the outdoors.

Why did I take such pleasure in killing woodchucks? Why do grown men shoot deer? Some say that by nature we like to exercise power. I remember the extension of self I felt when Uncle Sherwin blew the squirrel out of the great elm with a shotgun blast. I remember standing offshore on the deck of a salmon seiner out of Ketchikan, Alaska, and dropping a whitetail doe with a shot to the three inches of head exposed above a rock. Hitting a target gives only faint echoes of the reverberations of such an act.

Some say we carry by nature an aggressive charge which we must release as we can for growth and health. Some say we enter the world as mere potential, an unformed bundle of elements to which experience will give shape and meaning. We like to kill woodchucks and other living things only because we are taught to like it.

These notions, whether of power, discharge, exclusive nurture, or some other explanation, are deeply formative once they enter the popular mind. They begin as speculative forays into human nature, metaphorical flights of the poetic imagination of a biologist or dramatist or psychologist, but they end as received wisdom in popular discourse. Along with the rest of the nation, I have absorbed these messages, have put on these lenses through which I see the small woodchuck hunter and his dog. Even when most deliberately a traveler, I find it difficult to question the forms by which I have understood myself. It is not unlikely that even at age eight I enjoyed the exercise of power, and certainly my spiritedness sometimes tested the boundaries of civility. Whether either truly explains the pleasure of killing is less obvious to me.

Unquestionably I was taught to hunt. I read books, I heard the stories of my father and uncles, I saw deer hanging from trees in November, I came to prize the possession of weapons. Not long after this summer, I was given a .22 rifle and began to hunt with my father. Memories live in my body, my senses. I can still hear, in the sleepy dark of a deer season morning, the crinkle of waxed paper in which my father wrapped the cheese sandwiches, carried in his plaid wool shirt to be toasted over a midday fire in the November woods. The smell of linseed oil brings back the rifle stock I stripped and refinished. There is no richer blue than the blue-black of a gun barrel, no geometric form more intriguing than the rifle spiral. The thumping blast of a shotgun, the crack of a rifle are deeply satisfying sounds, and the blend of crisp autumn air with the pungency of burned powder penetrates the heart more sharply and deeply than any incense. But these experiences are more easily explained as the particular forms given to primary energies than as something completely manufactured out of elements with no character of their own.

I can confirm the fraternal and mythic imaginings of literature. I have owned a deer camp with other men. I have spent many hours with my father, uncles, and cousins, handling and firing guns, talking about hunting. I have even felt in a woodland clearing the presence of mysterious forces in the sudden manifestation of a deer, catching the light on its coat and disappearing as magically as it came, and I have seen big fish emerge from dark waters, taking shape as if some god were calling them into being out of imperceptible elements. How tentatively, though, must I use the word "confirm," for I cannot clearly distinguish that which I have been taught to see from that which I would have seen unaided. It is clear that I came to hunt because others had hunted before me, and they must have had their reasons. Even if one traced it back to necessity or to the belief that hunting strengthened the body and taught courage and cunning, these motives would not explain why it continued. It continued because of what it did to the heart.

As I try to reconstruct the context in which I took life with such delight, I realize that, on the farm, life as an abstract entity or force had only the dimmest existence, if indeed it so existed at all. It requires a special development of thought, alien to the productive, cultivating habits of the farm, to endow life itself with independent status. In keeping with the spirit of the farm and my own feelings, I did not take life, I killed woodchucks. Uncle Sherwin slaughtered cows and pigs. Even the religious foundation, God's act of creation, was not perceived so much as the creation of life as the creation of living things. There was no life independent of the forms in which it most obviously existed, no sacred abstraction to be violated if one killed an animal. Life was not a quantity or a principle. And even in human beings, life was that particular life, that man or woman who worked and loved and suffered. When Pauline Williams died, I lost not life, but Grandmother. And so, to kill things, the right things at the right time in the right way, seemed as natural as to help them come into existence; it was not an attack against life but a claim to some of the abundance of being.

Indeed, hunting and work were more closely related than might at first appear, for both domestic and wild animals existed for man's use and pleasure. If not for man, domestic animals would not exist at all in their present form. As for the wild ones, clean shooting was better than sloppy shooting, cruelty beyond that incidental to hunting was deplored (the founder even hated the supposed cruelty of horse racing), the grace and beauty of animal form and motion were much admired, and the mere presence of an abundance of wild animals made the world a more interesting and desirable place (except when they got into the crops); but for all that, it went without saying that man had a right to please himself by killing.

If our pleasures affect our sensibilities and perceptions, how does hunting affect the hunter's relations with other human beings? I suspect that there are fewer pacifists among hunters than among non-hunters, but both hunting and the acceptance of war may spring from a common source. Hunters are probably more willing than non-hunters to use force to protect their persons, family, and property. Familiarity with weapons probably disposes one to physical action, the extent and occasion of it depending in large part on other elements in one's situation and character. This may in turn contribute to a love of political independence, the expression of which also depends on local circumstances and character. The two classes of Americans most attracted to weapons are hunters and young outlaws. To the extent that my uncles and cousins are representative of hunters, the two groups could not be further apart in almost every other respect.

Although my uncles were gentle people, their familiarity with the death of animals helped them to accept the death of human beings as inevitable and natural; never in my memory did they speak of it as an absurdity or a flaw in the scheme of things. They accepted the order of life, as they understood it, and worked within it. All the same, when one of their number fell victim to nature's way, they cared for one another and grieved.

In some respects, their sensibilities were more delicate and refined than those characteristic of our time. Their entertainments were far less coarse and violent than those we routinely offer our children today. What they read about, saw on film, and heard on the radio was, even at its most extreme, mild and guarded compared to the celebration of sex and brutality seen every evening on national television. Perhaps, like most of the rest of us, they would have learned in time to indulge their potential for the vicarious satisfaction of bloodlust. It's strange to think that these hunters and farmers, who killed animals for pleasure and profit, would have been appalled by the pleasure succeeding generations have taken in brilliant imitations of the killing of people, while many of those who find hunting abhorrent allow their children to feed on this very fare.

For the private individual the ultimate question in this regard is the link between habits and character, for the citizen the link between habits and the fate of the nation. But Grandmother would have denied that the individual and the citizen could be separated. She might not have said that we needed to think about politics —the character of communities and nations—in order to think adequately about ourselves, but she would have agreed with the assertion that in shaping character we are also shaping the citizen. And she would have agreed that the deepest political conflicts are over what kind of people we want to be.

For some of us that question—what kind of person to be— has a disconcertingly long life. It was still alive for me many years after the farm when, quite by chance, I felt the experience of killing in a new way. That it should be fishing this time, rather than hunting, was of no importance. At the end of a day of work, I stopped my car by a small river, pulled on my hip boots, assembled the fly rod, and began to work the stream. The sun was low, the shadows long and dark. The only sounds were the steady murmuring of the current against the rocks and the slithering of the line through the ferrules. In this moment of utter concentration and expectation, I felt a trout strike the fly. It was a brown trout, not a big one, and it took only a minute or two to work him out of the current and ashore, but in that minute or two, I recognized something new. I felt what I had always felt when a fish struck and fought against rod and line, but the significance of the feeling, recognized for the first time, left me uncertain whether I would ever fish or hunt again.

What came over me in that brief, unequal struggle was that my sense of life became most intense at the moment of taking it. It seems obvious enough: there was a living being at the other end of the line. But it wasn't simply that. The life of the fish passed in vibrations through the line and rod into my hand, and from my hand to my hungry heart. The pleasure of artful killing in this instance was not the assertion of power or domination, not the release of aggression, and not a primitive ritual to placate or invoke a god, although of the three this last was the closest. It was the sudden, transitory satisfaction of the soul's craving for vitality as if, like a tree, it needed the nutritive sap or, like a motor, the electric current. The experience was vivid, grotesque, and somehow illicit. I wondered if violent crime, even some rape, had a similar source, not in the mere desire to hurt or to exercise power or release pent-up anger, but in the need to feel the resisting vitality of the other, as if only in that struggle could life be wholly present and accessible. Why, I wondered, do lovers imitate conflict and submission?

Some years have passed. The vividness has faded. I don't know if another fish on another day would recall the experience in anything like its original intensity. I doubt that it matters. What matters is less our experiences than what we make of them; they are either ends in themselves — achievements, satisfactions, defeats (dead ends, so to speak) — or doorways to something beyond. After all, there are experiences, complexly determined, over which we have little control, and our only freedom is in what we think about them.

Killing the trout was both a distinct experience — a stream of impulses along the nerves as immediate as sugar on the tongue or a lover's touch — and a step toward a larger view of how human beings place themselves in the world by exercising the full range of their powers. No person not radically crippled can avoid exercising all of them, but people are sharply distinguished by the proportions and spirit of their employment.

Like the barn cats and other animals, I took in the sights, smells, sounds, and touch of my surroundings and constructed out of them, with little conscious thought, a bounded and unified world. From earliest memory, however, I also desired things, things I could possess in tangible, physical ways to satisfy the various hungers of my nature. When I was thirsty I drank, when

I was hungry I ate, and the domestic economy was so designed as to satisfy these desires abundantly and ceremonially. The abundance acknowledged and legitimized the desire; the ceremony of manners and fixed times civilized it. On the farm milk came from the barn, meat from the slaughterhouse, potatoes from the field, and Grandmother prepared and served all according to custom.

In the first diary entry, I say I had two banana splits. Although I could not resist the hunger for food, I had to exercise some slight effort to satisfy it. The natural powers do not operate independently, for even so simple an act as eating requires a measure of force and thought.

From banana splits I moved to woodchucks, from the satisfaction of appetite to the exercise of spiritedness, my aggressive potential. My capacity and desire for action were now released to operate unfettered. So I hunted and in hunting may have felt something of that heightened sense of life so disturbingly present years later on the trout stream.

Nature appears to allocate this desire for the awareness of life most unevenly among human beings, both with respect to its quantity or intensity and to the characteristic means of its satisfaction. Then the desire is radically shaped by various disciplines of enhancement and restraint. In my engagement with the banana split, I felt a momentary concentration of attention and sensation that quite filled my universe, just as the lover, at the far end of the appetitive range, is filled with the delights of love. There are people for whom nothing quite equals the pleasures of the table. In killing woodchucks I put into play, with even greater passion, a quite different capacity. If the founder had been born into a noble Roman family, his natural vigor might have reached its highest pitch in the arts of rule and warfare. On the farm he recalled the heroism of his forefathers who cast off the British yoke, but was himself nurtured and constrained by quieter virtues.

Both appetite and aggression obscure the boundaries between the self and the other. The color of a carrot, the character of a lover, the gods of a city all dissolve in the act of possession or conquest. I was to learn that restoring the distinctive otherness of things requires action of a quite different kind.

A certain intellectual effort was required to hunt woodchucks. But I also read, I kept my diary, I observed and learned about the operations of the farm, and out of natural curiosity I took into my mind the features of my world, just as Aunt Ellrena's kittens did when they first explored the house. There was little that could be done without at least rudimentary thinking, and it was obvious, even to a child, that to bake pies, grow corn, and milk the cows required intelligence as well as desire and energy. The founder joined his faith in progress to the belief that "the supreme being made the earth for the use of man," but this God-given dominion could be properly exercised only through rational enterprise. Ingenuity was at the heart of it and one element of ingenuity was recognizing the nature of the materials, animate and inanimate, with which one had to work. To bend land and animals to his will, Uncle Sherwin had to know them.

But there was one more step. It was long after my summer on the farm that I came to recognize that, to some degree for all people and to a great degree for a few, there was such a thing as intellectual pleasure, ranging from simple curiosity to the passionate exploration of human nature and the world, in which the object is neither profit nor power nor the relief of man's estate. Here too man seeks dominion, but it is the dominion of inquiry and contemplation, which neither alters nor destroys.

For me as traveler, then, the ultimate value of banana splits, woodchucks, and trout is not what I felt or even learned when I first touched them, the unredeemed experiences, but what they can be made to reveal under the press of inquiry. I have put experience to the torture, although there are times when I wish that I were content to live in peace with what I have been and done. With a slight shift of perspective, an imagined acquiescence in the old ways, an obeisance at the family altar, the dust of travel floats away on the breeze. I become once more a true grandson, cousin, nephew, son, and citizen. But I am not content. I have tasted a confection sweeter than banana splits, have stalked game grander than the woodchuck. I did not heed the founder's injunction: "Let not our sons covet the western prairies or the gold of California . . ."

VI · Economics

He created all things for man.

But we must not forget that much of this increase of agricultural productions is owing to the increase and improvement in agricultural implements . . . Surely we are a people of progress, can we improve as much for the next half century.

HENRY LESTER, *Man Made for Agriculture*

I like to think of him [the founder] as an exceptionally smart man, shrewd as an old Yankee should be. How he got Mr. Hodges out of bed at midnight to make the last payment on this place, Grandfather having the money ready and anxious to pay before the date set, probably to save a little interest.

PAULINE WILLIAMS, *As I Remember*

I went down street with aunt Ellrena Gandma Uncle Sherwin and Larry. I had ten cents to spend but I could not find any thing that was worth it so I did not spend it.

Uncle Milo sold my papers and my magazines today. I got $1.65 for them.

I went up in the atti and got down some old books. I am going to sell them.

We followed the river up to the end of Uncle Milos properity.

CHARLES FISH, *Diary Book*

⊰⊱

Ownership meant, first, having those beautiful and useful instruments of the chase: my gun, my bow and arrows, and my knife. Next, it was having money, which I earned by nickel, dime, and quarter and carefully hoarded in a gleaming blue and white Raleigh's Ointment tin. I counted it so often that Grandmother said I would wear out the tin before the summer was over.

Money acquired a value of its own, dully gleaming, neatly stacked, heavy in the hand, and I was reluctant to part with it: "I had ten cents to spend but I could not find any thing that was worth it so I did not spend it." To this day, the notion of shopping as amusement is as foreign to me as potlatch or human sacrifice. Labor produced money but so did exchange; Uncle Milo sold some magazines I had collected and brought me $1.65. On another occasion, I took books from the attic to sell, but neither the diary nor memory reveals the outcome of that venture. I had learned some fundamental things about money and ownership. Money could be earned and it could be used to buy things, but if spent to buy one thing, it could not buy another. Frugality was one of the foundations of a good life.

One other lesson I learned about ownership that summer, or perhaps sensed rather than learned: to own clothes, a gun, an Indian headdress was one thing; to own a farm was another. Everyone had personal property, even the hired man, but only my uncles and their counterparts owned farms. I had walked with Grandmother to the end of Uncle Milo's "properity" and found the event worthy of writing down. Had I known the words, I would have said that boundaries were more than legal fictions, that the difference between "ours" and "theirs" characterized the land as surely as its ability to grow corn; but somewhat inconsistently I also felt that those boundaries were most believable that were marked by natural features such as brooks and wood lines.

But no matter how the lines were marked, there was something about the ownership of land that set it apart from other kinds of ownership, a certain something I must have absorbed from Grandmother and my uncles and which fed my later reflections. Farm ownership and farm work complemented one another, for both were immediate and tangible. What Uncle Milo owned was not an interest in something remote, but a physical reality he could see, smell, hear, touch, and walk on. Although sharing a corporeal nature with some personal property, it was far larger, more embracing and solid.

It was also permanent. Given a long enough scheme of things, this was of course an illusion, and even in recent geological time glaciers, beavers, floods, and man had changed the face of the farm. More recently still, the land had belonged to someone else before it came into this family. But for practical purposes, that is, for a sense of permanence, four generations (now six) are as good as eternity, and to step where one's great-grandfather stepped, to plow where he had plowed, is to be endowed with a feeling of continuity that in this country is rare. The land was forever, and family possession only a little less so.

They lived where they owned. The feeling of intimacy I have for the shirt on my back, a second skin, my uncles felt for the land. Rather than a distinct possession, the land—along with house, barns, machinery, and animals—comprised a whole that included belonging, pride, work, faith, hope, and fear. Their ancestors had planned and supervised the building of house and barns. The farm, then, was not only an economic unit; it was patrimony and legacy, something one legally owned but to which, in a different sense, one also belonged.

There was, of course, no primogeniture, no trace of the restrictions on inheritance which American law had long since abandoned, nor was there any significant social pressure to keep property in the family. If the farm and a few others like it were islands of continuity, they were surrounded by a vast sea of change in which the home place was as much a commodity as stocks and bonds. There persisted, nevertheless, another dimension of ownership, born of ancestral memory and the nature of the work, which conceived of the land as an extension of family, part of the family's understanding of itself and of the way it was perceived by others. Although there was no sacrificial hearth fire where the fathers' ghosts were fed, the conditions for such a conception existed in the texture of family life.

If ownership contributed to an inner sense of family, it also helped shape relations with the outer world. At a time when the economy of the town was more heavily agricultural than it is today, it seemed appropriate, even obvious, that farm families should take the lead in town government and local organizations. Except for higher taxes, the government demanded no more of its most prosperous citizens than of its poorest ones; there were not, as in ancient Greece, warships to be fitted out by private individuals or dramatic choruses to be trained.

Nor did ownership carry any official privileges. The family never asserted that because of its longevity or holdings it had more of a stake in the community than the next family, or any special claim to office. I did not hear the term "a stake in the community" until much later when I learned how property qualifications for voting and holding office had been gradually eliminated in the United States, and I felt the weight of opinion that such requirements were elitist, prejudicial, undemocratic. My uncles themselves would not have argued for them. In the social and economic facts of the farm and its town, however, I could see the roots of such a view, roots which flowered in my uncles' case in what the modern world calls "service." Of course, the farm family did have a stake in the community; the community was where it had lived for a long time, where it earned a living, where its children had been raised and educated, and where successive generations would get their start and perhaps make their lives. Gratitude, responsibility, and the love of one's own blended to make community service a worthwhile thing. No doubt the love of honor also played a part; Uncle Sherwin took pride in the many years he had held some of his offices. But here, too, moderation ruled, and political ambition was checked by a certain cultivated modesty as well as by the demands of the farm.

Finally, the land was not inert; to own and work it was not merely to manipulate mechanical elements to a given end. Although a jealous deity had long since driven out the river nymphs and no gods marked the boundaries, there was, I like to think, a hint of presences in the special places — the hemlock spring, the meadow brook, the big rock — that in other times would have been acknowledged. Now one comprehensive, ambiguous term had to suffice, so it was "nature" that one felt as snow melted, water ran, and the fecundity of the earth pushed green shoots into the sunlight. The sky my uncles did not own, but it was their sky where it covered the farm in a cape of blue or in swirling clouds and rain. And with these vital forces my uncles would cooperate when they could and contend when they must.

The farm was an island, but it was not a fortress, or not an effective one, and like most enclaves it carried within itself many of the traits of the world around it. The family would have agreed with the rest of the country that one of the inalienable rights inherent in the fee-simple ownership of property is the right to sell it. Like most farmers, they believed that their real wealth lay less in the farming business than in the appreciating value of their land, but of course that wealth could be extracted only if the land were sold or encumbered. Whatever attachment they might feel to the land and whatever position they might take on zoning, planning, and environmental regulation, they would correctly see that any move to restrict their ability to sell would deprive them of some of the value built up and tended over the generations. They had no quarrel with the profit motive, they believed in a market economy (government interference in the milk market might sometimes help but was viewed with suspicion), and they were frugal and prudent in all their dealings. They agreed with the founder's remark that the business should "replenish our pockets." Every animal on the farm had its price, Uncle Sherwin said. He was more reserved with regard to the land, but potentially that, too, could go. Sharing the basic economic and political principles of the rest of the country, but feeling in his blood the ties of accumulated experience, he lived in the hope that the farm would be home to his grandson and generations beyond.

I do not remember hearing the word "economics" spoken on the farm. My uncles and grandmother did not think of themselves as the objects of impersonal forces, obeying blind laws of valuation and consumption, nor did they look to a scientific discipline to shed light on their lives. They could not escape the workings of the larger economic order of which they were a part — milk and grain prices over which they had no control saw to that — but they gave their effort and attention to what lay at hand, taking care of what they owned, bringing "economics" back to its root meaning of the management of a household or an estate. Even the word "management" would have sounded a bit abstract except in its subsidiary sense of handling things — "we managed" — for management was part of work and no sharp distinction was made between planning and physical labor.

Although like all human beings they were ultimately driven by theory, it was theory absorbed, transformed into custom, habit, belief. Somewhere in ages past wise men spoke, and generations later, on a farm in Vermont, a family believed that man has a right to own property; that he must work; that he has an obligation to take care of his property for his own sake and that of his children and community; that he should do his best to take care of himself and not be a burden to others; that it is possible to love wealth too much but a greater danger is to be careless of it; and that no one will take better care of things than the owner whose fortune depends upon it. I never heard them say that "the eye of the master fattens the kine," but they lived as if they knew and believed it.

Of the two faces of economics, then, one looking in toward the immediate enterprise, the other out to the larger world, it was the former that I saw on the farm and that was most obviously present in daily life. My awareness of the other was limited to trips to the feedstore and the creamery. For the grown-ups, the larger world was always there but not always friendly: the grain check went out, the milk check came in, and on the relationship between the two depended the survival of the farm.

One of the frustrations of farm life is that it requires total responsibility of the farmer for the daily management of his property and business, but gives him virtually no power over what he pays and what he receives. No doubt many businessmen face similar difficulties, but unlike some the farmer is locked into a way of operating that can change only slowly if at all. The way he operates is largely determined by his investment in land, machinery, and animals; the market changes much faster than he can. Add a natural conservatism born of generations of habit and custom, and it is not surprising that many farmers show an amazing tenacity against great odds, then suddenly are no longer farmers at all.

The Biennial Reports of the Vermont Commissioner of Agriculture tell what has happened to the Vermont dairy farm since I was a boy. In 1944 there were in the state 296,082 milk cows, which produced approximately 1,215,022,516 pounds of milk. In 1989 there were only 163,000 cows, but they produced 2,225,510,565 pounds of milk. Using a different set of figures, perhaps more accurate, I find that in 1950 the average annual production per cow was 5,900 pounds; in 1965, 8,820 pounds; in 1980, 12,306 pounds; and in 1989, 14,337 pounds. (My uncles' farm averaged 8,000 to 10,000 pounds per cow in 1944.) The art of farming has always depended to some degree on the subsidiary art of herd improvement, but in modern times the dependence has accelerated, tying the farmer ever more tightly to the sources of technology and scientific research. Without good cows, a farm won't make it.

But production is not the only thing that has changed. In 1947 there were 11,352 dairy farms in Vermont; as of this writing, in 1992, there are 2,325. Fifty-six farms went out of business or were absorbed in the first six months of 1992. Only two years showed an increase: three in 1976, eleven in 1991. Losses in other years ranged from 21 in 1975 to 917 in 1966. At the same time, of course, production per farm increased, since the state's production increased by more than 70 percent even as the number of farms decreased by almost 80 percent. Pounds per farm per year went from 113,548 in 1947 to 878,260 in 1989.

This was not the first economic gale to blow through the lives of Vermont farmers. Remote Vermont hillsides, now heavily wooded, are laced with stone walls and cellar holes where farms once stood on clear land, the owners lured to the Midwest to grow up with the country. Except in a few river and lake valleys, topsoil in Vermont is a stingy skin over hardpan and rock. Photographs of local scenes from the last century are almost unrecognizable, there are so few trees. Even in my lifetime areas of the state have gone from about 25 percent forest to 75 percent as farmland has gone out of production. A century or more ago, Vermont hillsides were grazed by sheep, then by cattle; later the forests reappeared. "Our most useful domestic animals," wrote the founder, "are the horse, the ox, and the sheep." Compared to the history of agricultural communities in other times and places, the transformations have been rapid, driven by the engine of economic development at the heart of the modern enterprise. Compared to some other sectors of the economy, they have been slow.

To the family itself, a backward glance suggests a certain stability, an evolution of farming practice and family habits, the radical change occurring in 1965 when the cows were sold and the market garden became the sole and successful means of support. Even that left the land intact and productive, but now they were merchants as well as producers, linked in practice a little more closely to the commercial enterprises of the city, just as in terms of economic geography they grew closer to the expanding commercial districts of city and town. Some commercial establishments and housing developments have leapfrogged the farm, making it less a frontier between city and country and more an oasis.

Without laws or binding custom to dictate the use and disposition of property, the family faces two ways. The forces that counter the love of gain are mainly matters of the heart—family sentiment, an attachment to the past, a love of the land, a preference for a certain kind of independence. For me, the farm in memory is the farm in its quintessential form, abstracted from time, immutable, beyond profit and loss. Mere historical accuracy requires that I recognize it for something other than that, which I can easily do. The hard part is to tease out of the impacted reality of the farm its implications for community and for the course of my own life.

VII · Community

He [the farmer] must [be] thankful that the supreme being created him and ordained him for an agriculturist, placed him on a goodly soil in a good country, surrounded by a good society of his fellows.

Was it not the farmer that proclaimed the separation from the parent country, that we were a free and independent people, capable of self government?

HENRY LESTER, *Man Made for Agriculture*

In breeding horses as well as other animals, like are apt to beget and bear their like.

HENRY LESTER, *On Horses and Horsemen*

Strive to keep up the dignity of our name in our families.

MOSES LESTER, *A Dying Man's Letter to His Son*

Childrens day at Chapel today. I recited my piece. It was a good program.

The Fourth of July our nations birthday. We cerebrated the Fourth by haveing a picnic. I had a few caps left over from last year.

Daily vacation Bille [Bible] school ended today. For learning Bible verses they gave prizes. I received a prize, it was a black walnut letter opener.

CHARLES FISH, *Diary Book*

✂✁

Public and Private Places

Now and then, soaring high, I am brought to earth by unwelcome reminders of the reality of the physical world. No matter how exalted the flight, there is always a tether stretching down to a house or barn, a field, a village street. The mind may be its own place, but it inhabits a body, and the body inhabits buildings and a piece of the earth. Associations, pleasant and ugly, color my perception of things.

As apprehended from without, the farm was first and foremost a physical place, defined by the land, streams, trees, crops, house, and barns. From within, the physical features were no less defining but were infused with the particulars of long experience; they incarnated the hopes, fears, and principles of the family to whose life they were central. It was the same big rock from which the founder had split foundation stones, from which Grandmother, as a girl, had thrown green apples with a switch, where I picnicked as a boy, and next to which today the founder's great-great-great-grandson Paul plants corn. Every day I, a child, saw what Grandmother and my uncles saw, a house with a certain order and atmosphere, barns with a certain function, and over time I came to see them more or less as they saw them, in their representative value for the community's way of life.

If, fifty years ago, I had flown over the valley, I would have seen not only the Lester farm of my family but a liberal scattering of similar farms across the landscape. Imagining a way of life in its broad outlines, I could have said that people agreed that the most conspicuous monuments should be these private buildings devoted to the immediate physical and economic needs of their owners. The distances between farms and the fact that home and workplace were one would have suggested a political and emotional decentralization quite different from, say, the agricultural villages of the early New England settlers, who lived together in the shadow of the meeting house and went out to their land to farm. I would have acknowledged that for some purposes the nearby city was the center, that there one found public architecture on a significant symbolic scale, and that at one time, before my summer sojourn, town and city were one government. But in my childhood they thought of themselves as the distinct political entities they had become, and the farming community had a character of its own, determined only in part by its proximity to the city. Uncle Sherwin thought of himself as a man of the town.

To me, the boy, for whom the farm and its community were as permanent as the big rock or the land, the shifting patterns of history were mercifully obscure. But with the years came the awareness that the balance of public and private places as found in this little world was but one of many. I learned that the size and placement of the early New England meeting house said something about the community's conception of itself. The act of constructing it was both a religious and a political act, a statement about the ends of communal life. I began to think about ancient Greek temples, meeting places of men and gods; early American courthouses, temples of justice for the new republic; railroad stations and skyscrapers, symbols of commerce and enterprise; and, finally, shopping malls and the pseudo-physical space of television, palaces of consumption and a world of fantasy.

I find that nothing is more difficult than the familiar. Just as the farm, in its comprehensive immediacy, once appeared to be a natural world which revealed its intentions and artifice only under scrutiny, so too the dominant settings of a later time become more opaque as they become more commonplace. Nothing could be more obvious, that is, more physically apparent, than the eclipse of the church or meeting house as the prominent public space and its replacement by a succession of other politically revealing structures, including the megamall with its ambition to provide something like a total experience to the private individual. But to the shoppers the mall may be as natural a space as a farm to a farmer. They will have no reason to reflect that this most public of places is devoted to private pursuits. Amid an abundance of goods a king of old might have envied, they will not see themselves the subjects of a political experiment which has channeled their passions into a cycle of stimulated desire and satisfaction. They have what they want, they are post-political, and on their self-contained appetitive intoxication rests the security of the state. Such is the illusion.

Somewhere on the spectrum from temple to mall lies the farm. The patterns of land use, choice of buildings, and relationships between the domestic and the economic were all formed over time on the basis of political principles moving an entire nation, not just this single farm or this farming community. And so, to Grandmother and my uncles the prominent structures that most clearly represented the possibilities and demands of life were their houses and barns, and if they lifted up their eyes to the steep roofs or rising silo, it was to a vision there embodied of laborious independence, of self-reliance, and of the dignity of ownership. The farm was the place that really mattered, for there in one generous but bounded piece of land on which nature's gifts had been artfully shaped, were found both family and business enterprise. Whatever the economic and legal realities which linked this farm family to a vast system beyond, emotionally the farm was self-contained, providing scope for affections, ingenuity, and the love of struggle in the service of common goals.

Citizens and Leaders

Compared with the intense civic life of the ancient Athenians or the Puritan fathers, the life of the farm appeared to be private, but it was far different from the radically individual privacy of the urban throngs. The conditions of life combined with a tradition of agrarian thought to produce a political localism which emphasized the independence not so much of the individual as of the immediate group: first the family, then the town, and, at some increasing remove, the state and nation. The best government was the most immediate, and although Grandmother would not have called it government, it really began with the rearing of children and the management of the farm. Self-rule was clearly the most desirable kind and the conception of self was most vivid when confined to those selves whom the family knew and could judge. The self-rule of the entire state was more suspect because now the notion of self was much expanded to include people whose interests and principles might deviate from one's own. I remember the uncomplicated patriotism of the farm family. They were proud to be Americans, but the source of their pride was less what the United States as a central authority had achieved uniformly for everyone than what it made possible for small groups like themselves with the gumption to take advantage of their freedom. It was not a subject for intense analysis, but they believed that power exercised from afar was suspect.

In this combination of opinion and circumstance, active citizenship waxes or wanes according to the political scope left to local authority. When Grandmother was a young woman, local government was more powerful with respect to virtually every aspect of life: property appraisal and taxation, roads, education, public order, welfare. When she said she had lived frugally to avoid going "over the hill to the poorhouse," she had in mind an actual house, run by the town for the indigent. In my own lifetime I have seen a sharp curtailment of this authority in the interest of a more uniform justice. When Uncle Sherwin was a selectman, the Boards of Selectmen and the School Directors, the two governing bodies of Vermont towns, exercised considerable power under the general direction of the annual town and school meetings. Today, although their meetings are often stormy, selectmen and school directors are fighting over the remnants of a vanishing domain, for much of what they do is to administer the increasingly detailed agendas of the state and federal governments.

To a considerable extent the intended result is achieved: services are allocated more evenhandedly. But at the same time citizenship is diminished, if by citizenship is understood not merely a legal status, requiring only obedience, but participation in governing. As local government declines in importance, my cousins and their counterparts in the villages edge ever closer to the suburbanite or city dweller who carries to perfection the notion that one contributes to the public good by the exclusive pursuit of private interests. As farmers, doctors, or shopkeepers, much may be demanded of them; as citizens in the formal sense, very little. I suspect that their understanding of political questions also changes with the loss of power. Debated and resolved in distant forums, issues become abstract and one-dimensional, whereas they once affected friends and neighbors in immediate and perceptible ways. To the extent that deliberation over public ends and means can be a noble activity, one opportunity for noble action has eroded.

But the farm also had political limitations. My uncles, like many of their fellow countrymen, were very busy. Their work required them to be so and their moral tradition made it honorable. Whether leisure is a necessary condition of wise political action is not a question the world takes seriously anymore, so redolent is it of unearned privilege and elitist arrogance; but whatever the answer, participation in governing was for the farm both part-time and local. As power shifted from the towns, those who wanted to wield it had to follow. To seek the votes of strangers is different from seeking those of friends and neighbors. New skills are required, a different manner of address, more time. To deal with the increased complexities of a higher level of office, the leader must draw on resources of learning and experience that no one segment of the state or nation can give him.

Local politics was still important in Grandmother's time (and in some definite but limited respects it remains so today), but there was even then a significant loss of political confidence, of the belief that one's class and occupation uniquely fitted one for leadership on a grander scale. It had been many years since a farmer could echo with conviction the founder's declaration that upon the "true yeomanry" rested "the making and sustaining [of] our laws, moral, legislative, and national, and on their suffrages depend them that govern the states and the nation." Farmers could no longer dream of filling the "highest offices in the civil and military" and "being crowned with laurel as heroes, patriots and statesmen," as the founder says they once were in the republics of Rome and America.

All of these things posed a great challenge to any small community wishing to preserve a way of life that diverged significantly from the general drift of the greater society. For the farm to maintain its distinct character would have required a clear vision of what that character was, an equally clear perception of countervailing forces both within and without, and the ability to negotiate the differences between the two. It would have required moral ramparts and an intensive cultivation of the spirit within. It is not a feat that many groups have achieved except with the help of an isolation more extreme than that of the farmers of Vermont or of a moral and religious purpose more explicit and institutionalized.

The Arts of Cultivation

For Grandmother and my uncles nothing of its own nature would produce unaided the results they wanted. If they had been hunter-gatherers, a different case might be made, but even then they would have needed the primitive art of gathering and the more sophisticated art of hunting. They were not hunter-gatherers; if they hunted deer or picked wild blueberries, it was more for pleasure than for sustenance. Their farm was a place, but farming is a systematic action, an art; "to farm" is an active verb. Except as a piece of bounded earth or as idea, their farm did not exist independently of the arts it practiced. The earth is real and so, some would say, is the idea, but for incarnate form, the idea made manifest, the arts are necessary.

Although nature alone did not make the productive cows in Uncle Milo's barn, it was also true that the breeder's art worked with certain naturally given potentials and limitations. Part of the art was to recognize what these potentials were; the breeder could not make a silk worm out of a sow. At any given moment, the combination of existing technology, climate, animal and seed quality, soil characteristics, fertilizer, and human energy would set the limits of possibility. The best farmers, like my uncles, pushed toward those limits, seeking improvement, while the others did as they had always done, working habitually and achieving ordinary results.

Grandmother believed, as did the founder, that habit, custom, work, morality, and community life were inextricably connected.

Untutored human beings could not possibly grow up straight. To make a good man was to make a good worker and good citizen. If pressed to ask which of the three was most important, she would have said the good man, but would have clung to the opinion that the other two would follow.

What the farm understood so clearly is now unfashionable to maintain, that is, that no community can survive that does not cultivate the character of its citizens. Political independence, the arrangement of offices, and the structures of governing may survive, but communal values will not; eventually, for better or worse, a new soul will emerge in the old body. Almost by instinct people know this to be true. Even those who argue most vehemently for freedom of choice can seldom resist the urge to shape others according to their vision of the good life. The farm would not have put it so abstractly, but it would have agreed that at the heart of political dispute, once the more obvious passions are stripped away, we find competing visions of the good. Communities exist partly for physical security and material well-being, partly to live as their poets and seers have divined, and it is a commonplace of history that they will often sacrifice the former to the latter.

When the farm grew corn, the individual stalks existed only as indistinguishable components of a whole. Except in the simplest physical sense, Uncle Milo did not fertilize or cultivate individual plants; all were treated alike. Animals had some elementary individuality, but except as it affected production it was not significant. It was the kinds that mattered. The success of the enterprise depended on knowing the characteristics and needs of the various kinds of plants, animals, and materials which made up the working stuff of the farm. Uncle Sherwin could not handle hay as if it were sawdust, just as the woodworker must discriminate in purpose and treatment between pine and oak.

The first question for the cultivator of the human animal is whether he is dealing with stalks of corn, all of which can be treated alike, or with significantly different kinds of beings, although all of a single species. In the first instance, all the varieties of human character from sybarite to saint are socially produced. In the second, the cultivators are working with naturally given tendencies or inclinations or potentials which vary from person to person. In this view, it is the right match of nature and nurture that produces the richest blooms.

A true community would know its own character, that is, would have an established way of life that fostered those traits it most esteemed. It would resemble the farm at its most spiritually vigorous. If it were lucky as well, the traits it fostered would be appropriate to its place in the world and would support and preserve the community. If it were more than lucky, it would understand the range of human types and would have a place for them. But human types are incarnated in human beings who seek wealth, fame, power, or knowledge, and who would arrange things — or destroy things — to satisfy their wants. So to cultivate is not only to fertilize but to weed and prune as well. And there is no fertilizing, weeding, or pruning without some vision of the good.

Achieved Character

It is the virtue of small, sharply defined communities that they know what they want to perpetuate; they produce clear results in a narrow band of the spectrum. It is their weakness that other possibilities are ignored or suppressed. It is the virtue of large, open communities that nearly every human type can find a niche in them. It is their weakness that in their fluidity they lose focus and direction, they waste talent, and they abandon the responsibility of cultivation to random social forces.

The farm bred responsibility. As in many kinds of work,

attention and precision mattered. A fence could be perfect for half a mile, but a three-foot gap would let the cows out. Cows had to be milked twice a day, every day, year after year. Uncle Sherwin and Aunt Ellrena went on occasional short vacations, but they could not simply take a day off now and then. The information printed on the inside covers of the old record book I used for a diary — helpful hints for farmers, weights and measures, basic legal principles — captured the spirit of the factual, tangible world of the farm. The responsibility was intensified and heightened by the fact of ownership. The men and women were not following orders; they were carrying out their own decisions and plans on which the success of the undertaking ultimately depended.

It was obviously more than an occupation. Engaging the entire family, demanding the utmost exertion, and drawing upon a heritage of agrarian self-respect, farm life absorbed the time, energy, and thought of its people. This contributed to the formation of character — made it easier to see what kind of character was needed — and helped form a community in the strict sense of shared essentials. At the farm's peak, responsibility was responsibility to the family and the farming enterprise in the light of a certain moral and religious understanding. The journey of man was a fixed path. The particulars could not be foreseen, but the conduct of the journey and the ultimate destination were clear. Except as inheritors who took what had been given them, the family did not have the responsibility of choosing a way of life. That one could study deep alternatives — not just employment but radically different destinations — was not a temptation that circumstances dangled before them. That such study might call into question inherited opinions of the nature of man, of duty and fulfillment, of political order and justice would have struck them as a threat to the good life.

In language much out of fashion now, I think of the farm as

favoring manly and womanly characteristics which were sharply distinct in some respects, rather close in others, a division of labor within a common purpose. In the capacity for hard work, men and women were similar, but with few exceptions they worked at different tasks, recognized their separate domains, and did not compete. Both had to perform repetitive, physically demanding jobs day after day, and it was considered a sign of good character to do so efficiently and cheerfully. Men were allowed a certain latitude in speech and demeanor; women were expected to stay within a more limited, modest range. Production, physical maintenance, and negotiating with the outside world were largely in the men's province, although, as I've said, Grandmother, as well as Uncle Milo, lent money at interest for extra income. House decoration, flowers, needlework—all the beautiful things—belonged to the women as, of course, did cooking, mending, washing, sewing, cleaning—all the housework. Resourcefulness was prized in both—how to cope with emergencies, repair things, make do with less. Grandmother was fond of the old maxim:

Use it up, wear it out;
Make it do, or do without.

Loyalty to each other, to the family, and to the common enterprise was assumed and did not need to be discussed. Steadfastness, endurance, and a kind of defensive heroism were found in both, and in my imagination reached their most dramatic expression at the time of the great flood.

The farm wanted in its men a tempered spiritedness, in its women a tempered affection. The tyrannical man was as much an aberration as the timid or listless one. The indulgent mother was as subversive of good order as the harsh one. A good meal, a nap, rocking, a night's sleep, listening to records, sitting on the porch of an evening, growing flowers, a bucket of switchel in the hayfield — these I remember as concessions to sensuous pleasure. I doubt that for six generations on the farm a man or woman ever made a practice of lying in the sun at a beach or even in the backyard.

In everything it was the middle ground the farm sought to occupy, the decent mean, the workable whole, an emotional and spiritual sobriety. The powers and passions of the individual were restrained and blended by precept and habit to form a kind of balance in which no element was completely starved and none grew fat and sassy. Whether such a balance was a kind of harmony depends on what music one can hear; there were distant rhythms, barely perceptible, which never became thematic. To make money was necessary to the entire enterprise, but nobody dreamed of making a lot. The scale of the operation imposed certain financial limits, which were accepted as a natural part of life. To waste money or to lust for great riches would have been equally eccentric. Even the founder, who acquired nearly 600 acres in three towns before he died, exhorted the Vermont farmer to cultivate better his own land rather than buy his neighbor's, and down to the present day his real estate purchases are regarded as slightly out of character for the family.

The farmer, then, was not a pure type and farming was a mixed way of life. Farming called into play reason, spiritedness, and love of gain, but could not allow unbridled expression to any of them without jeopardizing the farm or changing the farmer into something else. The proper use of reason was to oversee the operation of the farm and to keep oneself in harmony with practical necessities and with the moral and religious teachings of the family; it was not to question those teachings or to search out the why of things. Spiritedness, the aggressive, competitive, honor-loving element of human nature, was confined to the unending struggle of farm work and to local politics; unchecked, it would have tyrannized over this little world or would have demanded a larger and more contentious field of play. And the love of gain, which served the desire for comfort, pleasure, and safety, could not range beyond the limits imposed by the economics of farming; to have desired more grandly would have taken the farmer off the farm or would have transformed the farm into a different enterprise. A more pronounced love of sensuous pleasure would have interfered with the intensity and regularity of farm work and would have violated the moral and religious principles which guided the family.

In short, an excessive development of the natural powers was as dangerous as their deficiency, and pure types, or approximations thereof, were either threatening or comical. If a man crossed the line between hard bargaining and sharp practices, he became a rascal. A lecher hovered in public opinion somewhere between the contemptible and the ludicrous, a victim of his own nature. The farm had not reached the stage of tolerant accommodation enjoyed by a more modern farmer of my acquaintance, who said of womanizing, "It's a small fault in a good man." It was assumed that without obedience to the traditional restraints which direct and limit the exercise of the fundamental powers of the individual, the community would sow the seeds of its transformation or destruction.

In the family and farming community, as well as in the individual, a steady state was the unspoken goal, accommodating various needs without excessive attention to any of them. Economic and political decisions were made in the same spirit as moral ones. Roads were what they had to be to allow traffic to move; they had begun as narrow gravel strips, and with time most were widened and many were paved. Bridges had to carry vehicles over rivers. The old covered bridges, not splendid monuments but handsome in their way, were succeeded by the much plainer, more practical concrete bridges of no architectural distinction whatsoever. When the old barns, with their gambrel roofs and massive mortised and tenoned timbers, succumbed to fire or rot, they were replaced with much simpler, more efficient buildings, which will excite no admiration in later generations. But even the original barns were designed to be practical, and it took many years and the awareness that they belonged to a vanishing era for them to acquire the sentimental and representative value they have in our minds today. It saddens me to see the deterioration of the farm's big hay barn, but the lack of maintenance was calculated. The schools taught what the young needed to know to become like their parents and over three generations moved from one-room schoolhouses to modern brick-and-glass structures, mainly because of state and federal standards. When I was a boy, part of the lower level of a schoolhouse was enough for the town offices, which now occupy nearly the entire building. The most conspic-uous public building in the neighborhood was the chapel, and that wasn't public in the governmental sense. Just as the individual farmer did not aspire to be king or tycoon or landed aristocrat, the town did not aspire to be Athens.

There was not, indeed, any public determination that the town should remain an agricultural community, although at one time it must have seemed to almost everyone that it was natural and proper for it to do so. The town as a town had no such official understanding of itself. Indeed, under existing political arrange-ments, it could not have, except for certain tax relief measures for farmers, which it did in fact pass when many of the farms had already disappeared, many years after my summer on the farm. Farms survived or died by individual decision in response to changing economic conditions. There was much public sentiment in support of farming as a way of life, but no effective political program for maintaining it. In most respects, the powerful agents of preservation or change had ceased to be local.

Community Ends

As I think about the changes in the farm and the wider world, I ask myself how long any community can remain strong, vigorous, and determined without believing that its gods are the true gods, without some vision of life that inspires devotion and guides thought and action. At one time this question would not have been an uncomfortable one for democratic societies to entertain, but today it threatens to intrude into the ever-expanding private realm. Grandmother would have agreed with the once familiar argument that democratic government requires the greatest degree of hard work and self-restraint on the part of its citizens, and that one of the responsibilities of government is to encourage these virtues. She would have been most uncomfortable with the re-definition of democracy as the neutral guardian of private choice in child rearing, sexuality, family relations — indeed in much of what we call morality. What we would consider today as intrusion into the private sphere she would have considered legitimate authority to perpetuate a way of life. She would have said that of course we can legislate morality. We can and we do. She might have seen that virtually all legislation is ultimately the legislating of morality, since the choice of this or that rule or law is ultimately a moral preference. Morality undergirds legality.

Some of the most vexing features of democratic society were seldom if ever felt as questions or issues on the farm. My awareness of social class goes back to my observation of the farm's gentle hierarchy — Uncle Milo and Grandmother, Uncle Sherwin and Aunt Ellrena, Larry and Gareth, the hired men — but this arrangement and its harsher analogues in the outside world were seldom subjects of comment. The farm did not think of itself as a stage in the progress of equality or liberty. It had found a workable balance in that aspect of our social relations in which our principles and passions tend to be most confused — our experience of relative merit and esteem. The principle of equality is bred into us, but we pride ourselves on our intelligence, beauty, status, and successes.

The position of the hired men on the farm is the earliest instance of the subtleties of inequality that I can remember. Although I could not have explained it, it gave me a glimpse of the fact that people are different, sometimes in fundamental ways, and that their differences lead to finely graduated differences of attitude. Because all this was simply a fact of life on the farm, requiring little if any discussion, it was not until much later that the obvious occurred to me, that it is a question of no small magnitude how far and in what way the consequences of these different attitudes should be subject to law and to what extent the customs of the land should be bent to alter the attitudes themselves. As the dream of equality has penetrated ever more deeply into our hearts, it has grown ever more incapable of realization, for it has become nothing less than the dream of *feeling* equal, an inner consciousness that one is at least as good as everyone else, in every significant way.

The workings of these passions were long obscured to me by the deep moderation and restrained manners of the farm and of my own family. For all their independence, Grandmother and my uncles were guided by a certain deference toward talent, achievement, and position, perhaps born of their Christian heritage. The farm's hierarchy did not reveal the complications such an arrangement might entail among people less thoroughly or differently disciplined. It took years of experience in a much different world, as well as a more critical examination of my own heart, before I came to understand that the question of equality is a tangled one, leading directly into the thicket of envy, emulation, jealousy, guilt, pride, belonging, and exclusion.

The old revolutionary battle cry was liberty, equality, and fraternity. When Uncle Sherwin and Aunt Ellrena went to the chapel for a supper with their neighbors, they were enjoying the company of a small band of like-minded people. They did not have to speak of fraternity; they lived it. In any community convinced of the rightness of its ways, there must be some feeling of superiority; fraternity implies exclusion as well as inclusion. But whatever advantages the farm may have enjoyed, it enjoyed quietly. Grandmother and my uncles were not moved by missionary zeal, threatened by oppression, or worried about their rights. They had their place in the world and were comfortable in it. They certainly wished to "keep up the dignity of our name," as the founder's father advised, but status was not something they worried about.

Not so for those for whom the compelling question is rights, not obligations, and whose status is uncertain. Once the idea of equality is entangled with the pain of inferiority and the desire to surpass, it becomes not merely a principle but a passion. Human beings, like the animals on the farm, seek the pleasure of rubbing together; the need to belong is expressed daily in a million lunch booths across the land. But for many people, perhaps to some degree for all, belonging is not enough; one must also stand out, distinguish oneself. If the measure of such satisfaction is simply individual achievement or gain, independent of some larger purpose such as animated the farm at its strongest, the struggle has a curious way of souring the spirit, perhaps because there is no measure of how much is enough.

Although the farm would have considered it just and prudent to try to establish certain kinds of equality, it would have recognized the task as impossible with respect to beauty, intelligence, skill, and self-esteem, and next to impossible with respect to wealth, political power, and social status. It would have seen that only in fraternity comprehensively understood—associations devoted to ends superior to their members—and even there most uncertainly, does equality have a chance to be felt in the blood and bones, for only there is one's worth a gift of the heart rather than a genetic accident or the victor's crown.

If moderate in its expectations for equality and fraternity, the farm, as mentioned above, would have been even more restrained in its opinion of liberty, recognizing that liberty becomes more problematical as it becomes more individual and personal. It is one thing to want one's country to be free of foreign domination; it is another to want free, that is, democratic, institutions within one's country; and it is yet another to want personal freedom in whatever one considers the most significant parts of life. When the founder spoke of independence, he thought of an independent "profession" or "class" and therefore of a way of life in which religion, virtue, and self-government could flourish. He did not imagine the extent to which independence or freedom would become a personal matter, not only allowing a wide range of individual choices but assuring an inner conviction of freedom as well. We even imagine that the law can free us from the common afflictions of the race, as indeed in some instances it can; we speak of our right not to be hungry, cold, homeless, jobless, assaulted, or even, for certain reasons, insulted. Sporadic as these benefits are in the history of mankind, the demand for them does not startle or amaze. Only our failure to make them widely available stirs our political passions.

Since my immediate family was more simply a family in the contemporary sense and much less an enterprise, it was the farm which gave me my first glimpse of a coherently ordered association, combining a wide range of human interests in service to a common end. Although not something the farm would try to articulate, except allusively and indirectly, it was the common purpose that justified the simple hierarchy as well as other limits on human relations.

To what extent, if at all, various hired men understood the purpose and thought of themselves as serving it and not merely their own financial needs, as the more fortunate slaves of Athens are said to have served the city, I cannot say and will never know. I do know that from an early age I was aware of the amusement occasioned by their quirks and foibles, amusement that people comfortable in their superiority feel in the presence of their inferiors. By that sign and, no doubt, many others, including the room the men occupied and the way they spoke, I began to notice rank and status and was taking in, all unconsciously, some of the stubborn facts of human difference, which pose the gravest questions for political thought and practice.

Once again it is the familiar that is the hardest to grasp. Under the spell of the poets and thinkers who ushered in the modern world, we live in the realm of the personal and the individual. We have come to think that we own ourselves, that we may do what we want with ourselves, that fulfillment, not right action, is the end of life, and, paradoxically, that the highest duty is to protect the rights of others so that they may live in a manner equally independent and individualistic. That community might constitute a suprapersonal entity to which we would belong and whose interests would outweigh our own is a concept increasingly difficult to understand and accept.

In Grandmother's mind existed an ancient notion of religious and moral obligation which, if pressed, she would have declared compatible, perhaps identical, with citizenship. Such views have become radicalized and now most obviously characterize the "religious right." For many of the more intellectually fashionable groups, God is dead or missing, and the possibility of a corporate life that would rescue us from a consuming individualism grows ever more remote. We hunger for community, the word is much on our lips, but we live in a world of anxious individualism, political and psychological, that makes community in any profound sense difficult to achieve.

Continuity and Change

However obviously the externals of her world were changing, at its foundation — what Grandmother considered to be good and true — there was a bedrock of meaning and purpose of which her determination and steady habits were the moral reflection. A floor swept in support of a way of life was not the same as a floor swept in the mere interest of cleanliness. The farm in general and Grandmother's life in particular embodied that continuity without which there is no community. Whatever it is that unites people, that constitutes an association, must persist; otherwise the community dissolves or re-forms itself on different principles.

Cohesive and determined as it was, the farm was never in its practices and principles as detached from the larger society as, say, a monastery, nor was it as deeply governed by custom as some isolated, so-called primitive peoples. In the regularity of its workday, the ceremony of meals, and the general good order of its domestic arrangements, it may have hinted at the holy hours of monastic discipline. And in the repeated experience of generations on the same piece of ground with the same distinctive features — the fertile soil, the ever-flowing river, the intimate meadow brook, the swimming hole, the big rock, the cedar spring, the house and barns — the family reenacted as in pantomime the sharply circumscribed, intensely local drama of societies more profoundly traditional than itself. Only as ghosts or shadows did the tutelary deities manifest themselves in meadow and spring; the special places were visited but not quite occupied.

It was more than kinship, then, that drew me back to the farm, more than the recognition that its blood ran in my veins and would forever be part of me. That alone would have made the farm a necessary stop on my journey, but it was this mixed state, this uncertain status between a separate community of virtue and the world at large, that gave it particular value for my inquiry into the ambiguities of individuality and community.

Grandmother and my uncles saw clearly the artfulness of farming. Close to the natural rhythms of seasons and weather, intimately aware of the signs and consequences of animal health and disease and of the characteristics of the land and the living things it supported, they never suffered the delusion of sentimental outsiders who imagined an easy harmony between farmer and nature that would cure mankind's ills. If the distinctiveness of the farm's way of life were to slip from their grasp, the cause would not be a failure to understand what was necessary to support it economically. And there was much else to preserve it: loyalty to past generations (no generation had ever rebelled against its predecessor), the blending of home and workplace, the belief that the farming life had served one well and would do the same for one's children. If some most unlikely revolution had decreed that family land could not be sold, there would have been much in the experience of the family to support it.

But interwoven with the family pieties were strands of a different hue. Change, to Uncle Sherwin, was a law of life. "The times are changing," he would say. Simple and obvious words, and although he did not intend them to apply to the realm of principle and duty, they came from deep within him. Change meant uncertainty, and uncertainty hung over the farm just as it did over the more turbulent life of the city. When the founder spoke of progress, he imagined an even more productive agriculture, but to Uncle Sherwin progress might include some other use of the land. It was obvious to him that land was money. For most farmers no other asset, certainly not the business itself, could equal the accumulated value of the land. At one imaginative extreme the land was the home of family gods, at the other a commodity like soap or gasoline. The head knew how the world reckoned; the heart was divided.

It was obvious that the farms that survived did so not because of family feeling but because of superior management and technology. Management and technology were the hallmarks of the larger social order and economy. The very changes that enabled one to prosper on a farm, therefore, were small steps away from a distinctive, traditional way of life. While the economic and technological order, of which the farm as a business was a part, grew more complex and denser, the spiritual order, of which the farm as a way of life was a part, grew weaker and thinner.

On the farm and beyond, it was obvious that better seed, bloodlines, and machinery required hard work, clear goals, trained intelligence, and institutional support. In my memory it was Grandmother who saw most clearly that the moral and spiritual life required something like the same. She saw it and tried to treat her family accordingly. In true Protestant fashion, the locus was the individual soul, not the church or any highly developed cult or ritual. Except in the broadest and loosest sense, her religion was not institutional. The local chapel was important to those who attended and supported it, but it was not identified with any denomination, it did not represent any sharply defined creed, and it exercised little influence over the people independent of what they, through meeting there, exercised over each other. She may not have felt the lack — I suspect she did not — but while sharing the same aspirations for posterity as those of more structured and institutionalized traditions, she had to make do with much less in the way of social organization and public symbols. No Chartres or Notre Dame for her, not even a big white church with a black-robed preacher and choir. Although the soul of the farm was formed by a combination of forces, ancient and modern, from well beyond its borders, its vigor and definition depended in large part on the receptivity and devotion of each successive generation. While the same could be said of any association, the absence of a rich panoply of custom and ceremony made the dependence especially critical.

The farm occupied an intermediate niche between, say, the family of very early Greece, fundamentally a religious association devoted to the family gods, and the most extreme type of modern family, formed out of passion and affection with no clear purpose beyond pleasure, the perpetuation of the line, and the preservation of family feeling. Passion and affection stir the soul, but unless they are linked to duties and less immediate aspirations, they do not provide much ballast. A great many families do not complete the voyage. As communities, including the national community, come less and less to embody principles in the service of which we can rise above the limitations of our private worlds, Americans find themselves increasingly hungry for deeper associations even as they cling to their independence and resist anything that smacks of coercion.

The cry for community, like the memories of family, is often sentimental. Sentimentality, a cynic remarked, is the lie by which families and communities are held together when common purpose fades. Just as family sentimentality is selective memory, screening out the bitter to enjoy the sweet, so community sentimentality is the illusion that we can have solidarity without losing anything else we have come to cherish. We want the psychological benefits without the substance of the thing itself. People who live in vigorous communities don't want "community"; they want to display their excellence or kill enemies or punish sinners or serve the gods — sometimes all four. Community follows.

Privacy, individuality, self-fulfillment (as commonly understood) are not necessarily incompatible with community — there have been strong communities that allowed a fair measure of them — but they move the soul in a different way; they are agents of change, not continuity. It might not be true under a harsh despotism, but in our circumstances to wish for more privacy, more individuality, and more self-fulfillment is to wish for less community.

VIII · The Farm and Beyond

Man was made a social being and for agriculture and those arts connected and necessary thereto belonging. Let him not therefore repine and be unsatisfied with his lot, but cheerfully and industriously submit to act in the sphere for which he was created.

HENRY LESTER, *Man Made for Agriculture*

Dear Son, I would have said a few words more to you the other day, but I am so deaf it was not convenient. My health is very poor, and I have so many infirmities about me I must soon be gone. It is wonderful I have been spared so long, I hope for a wise purpose. God knows best; I wait his time.

My health is failing daily, and your health now is no security against death. Let us be prepared for the solemn hour is the fervent prayer of your affectionate father.

MOSES LESTER, *A Dying Man's Letter to His Son*

Grandma [the founder's wife] lived a great many years after her husband's death, patiently waiting, knitting, ever knitting, until the time came for her to put it aside, and go into the great beyond.

PAULINE WILLIAMS, *As I Remember*

❧❧

For Grandmother life was a pilgrimage, with heaven its destination. Like her great-grandfather, Moses Lester, she was "prepared for the solemn hour," and although she took seriously the things of this life, they were ultimately instrumental. Since the final measure of worth was not of this world, she could live confidently and serenely, more at home in her pilgrimage than those feverish souls for whom this world is all and whose hopes and fears are at the whim of fortune. She was the least alienated of beings. Principle and affection bound her to family and community even as she imagined a whole of which they were but transitory parts.

As I review the course of my life, I see a more irregular path. At times I could not see the direction, to say nothing of the destination. In the geography of my travels, family and farm are at the center, not only at the center of my experience but at the center of social and political life. For many people — it could have been true for me — the circles of association from family to nation are an unbroken expansion of territory, opportunity, affection, and loyalty. Time and experience never breaks that narrow boundary within which their life begins; it only pushes it wider. But such is not the case for all.

From earliest childhood, I enjoyed the embrace of family; I knew what it was like to feel at home, loved and cared for. In time I began to imagine how a man might live, what he might do both to please himself and to win the admiration of others. For

years it was unthinkable that one might define oneself in oppo-
sition to the community or chart a direction the community did
not acknowledge; the people I knew and loved did not stray.
Secure within the charmed circle, I grew to admire the determination and buoyancy of the practical men and women who
exercise dominion, who plant and harvest, build and preserve.
Men like Uncle Sherwin and Uncle Milo address the demands of
the day with vigor and confidence. Their devotion is obvious, if
seldom spoken, and they display a manly bearing a boy might
imitate. The good they do is immediately apparent, and they win
the affection of those whose lives they support and protect.

Later I learned that in political life, power and loyalty can
support larger purposes, and I was moved by the dedication
and ability of the best of those men and women who serve the
common good. It takes a more experienced eye to see how they
too plant, harvest, and preserve — their efforts are more often
ambiguous and debatable — but it was clear to me even as a
young man that to do their job well they need to be intelligent,
courageous, and persuasive. I admired these characteristics; I
wanted them for myself. And as I earned my share of recognition
on the job or in school, I discovered how sweet honor is. Like
the planters and protectors of my childhood, these public men
and women live within the circle, loyal to a way of life whose
fundamental principles they do not question. Their reward is
honor.

Then I discovered that there are people for whom the deepest
satisfactions of life are very different. For them the things of this
world are most compelling as subjects of inquiry and contemplation. They are the seekers and knowers, vigorous in their conquest
of the unknown but gentle in possession. Trying first to understand
and only then, if at all, to change and control, they ask why a
flower turns toward the sun, why one country thrives while another declines, why some children grow tall and straight and

others are stunted and bent. They ask what is good, beautiful, and true. Nearest to their quest in my childhood, but not the same, was Grandmother's love of her garden or my mother's love of poetry. The seekers often make no stir among their neighbors; they live quietly and obediently. But where others find certainty, they see questions; where others act, they observe; where others are rooted, they roam. In their hearts, many are restless; some are exiles.

There was little in my childhood to suggest that I would join their company. I was not only comfortable in the confines of my upbringing, I enjoyed playing a part. As a boy, I learned to charm and persuade, a skill dependent upon a sense of place and the people. When I delivered newspapers, I expanded my route; when I worked at an A&P store, customers went home with heavier shopping bags and lighter wallets. It became second nature to divine character and opinion in the rhythms of speech, the turn of a phrase, or the expressions on a face. In part I was reading individuals, but I was also responding to the moral and social forms of the community.

My ease and skill began with the intimacy of the farm and my sense of two worlds, the bounded one of the farm with its familiar manners and practices, and the strange, unbounded one beyond. The diary reports meetings with the outside — the highway with the truck driver who swore; the city with hospital, stores, and dump; the newspaper stories of a homicidal maniac on the loose — but except for a passing sense of the exotic, a momentary fear, the diary does not reflect any threat to the primacy, legitimacy, or security of the farm. As physical setting, enterprise, and family, the farm held and protected me. The sun on the barnyard in the morning, the shade of the ancient elm, the rumble of the ensilage cart, the cows' breath in the cold air — these things gave me a place. In contrast to the peripheral and foreign character of what lay beyond, the farm was all the more obviously the warm center of the universe. When I visit there even now, with many of the people gone and the larger life pressing more heavily, I feel inside again.

The people within were one's own. They were not chosen, they were given, and they could no more be exchanged for a better lot than one could exchange one's face or arms. Marriage was for life. Some marriages were lucky, some were not, but that was beside the point.

Because this life was bounded and its parts interconnected, it gave the illusion of permanence. As a boy on the farm, I woke to the same world I fell asleep in. Even now, idly musing, I can bring back the dead to a summer morning, the farm astir, and feel as if the half century gone had never been. Somewhere deep within, the roof line of the big barn runs straight, cows graze in the pasture, horses move at Uncle Sherwin's command, and Grandmother brushes the dinner crumbs off the table. There is morning, noon, and night but no calendar showing the flight of years.

Stability had consequences. Even as the scene changed, there was always a world in which I felt strong and at home. As I grew older, the boundaries expanded until they included the realms of work, of public affairs, of groups and institutions, of struggle, contest, compromise, resolution, and achievement. There were women in it, but I grew up to think of it as a manly world in which the manly virtues counted. I could chair a meeting, negotiate a bargain, forge an alliance, teach a class, endure enmity, go without sleep, lose a career and find another.

When after years "away," as my family called any place outside Vermont, Eleanor and I returned to the state with our son, Andrew, we bought an old farmhouse in the small hilltop village of Dummerston Center where, except for an occasional owl, the nights were so quiet we could hardly sleep. The house came with four acres, all that remained after repeated land sales, a dismantling common to Vermont farms.

The boundaries of these four acres were quickly toured. To the south I found neighbors whose love of their native state brought them back despite a job that took the husband around the world. Their deep lawn merged with meadow, which in turn gave way to woods and a ravine through which ran a small brook. Here, when Eleanor was pregnant with Justin, Andrew wandered away and in the hour it took to find him we imagined that we would lose and gain a child the same day. Crossing the brook and partway up a hill, I came to the east boundary, which was flanked by a cemetery with stones dating back to the eighteenth century. On one stone I read:

> *Blessed are the dead*
> *That live in the lord.*

On another:

> *My flesh shall slumber in the ground*
> *Till the last trumpets joyfull sound*
> *Then burst the chains with sweet surprise*
> *And in my Saviour's image rise.*

Children were buried there, many children, and veterans of the American Revolution. Among the dead I found names as long familiar in this town as Lester and Williams in Rutland.

I followed the north boundary up the slope through the meadow, past the big butternut tree, a rare walnut, and the new raised ranch of the family from whom we bought our house, and on to the road. Along the road to the south, a stand of pines,

maples, and locusts gave the poison ivy the partial shade on which
it thrived.

Across the road to the west stood the parsonage — two-
storied, old, sturdy — joining most of the other village houses with
its white clapboards and green shutters. Our house, a fading,
peeling red, was one of the exceptions; later we stained it brown
in quiet defiance of local custom. Also across the road was a
neighbor who grew apples and strawberries and made maple
syrup. From our windows we could see the steam billow out of
his sugarhouse; at night the sparks rode the wind. Another neighbor had served as town clerk for over forty years; when she retired
in 1973, she was only the fourth clerk since 1812.

Nearby were the church, Grange Hall, firehouse, and town
office building. Andrew and Justin caught frogs and crayfish in
the firehouse pond and picked wild blackberries behind our house.
Old apple trees and pear trees attracted deer and, once, a mother
bear with her cub. From a mountaintop a short hike away, we
could see Mount Snow and Stratton Mountain in the ski country
to the west, Mount Monadnock in New Hampshire to the east.
Below, a silver path in the distance, the Connecticut River ran
through our valley on its passage from Canada to the sea.

In this village, as in an expanded circle of the farm, our lives
unfolded. Here our sons grew to manhood. Eleanor watched over
their homework and drove them to ball games, lessons, the doctor.
We planted flowers, grew our own vegetables, joined the PTA,
went to school concerts.

I taught at a nearby college and later, when it closed, went
into business. I became a volunteer fireman, served on charitable
boards, joined clubs, and was elected school director and selectman. Moving with ease through the intricacies of local business
and politics, I was reminded of how much men love honor; I loved
it myself. I watched businessmen and politicians cry when the

crowd rose to applaud them. The pleasure they derived from power and position was not the pleasure of ordering people around. The tears they shed when honors came were not tears of triumph; they were tears of gratitude for affection received and for reassurance that they had done well. Theirs, too, was a bounded world; they lived within it and had their reward.

For me as husband, father, citizen, man of the town, there were no sharp discontinuities between the farm and this house and village where I now write. Although the farm of fifty years ago and the village of today differ in many ways, I moved from one to the other by a series of steps that in retrospect had an inner coherence despite the absence of a plan. But I am writing, carried, as a boat is carried, by currents of thought that grow ever stronger. Even in the years that business most absorbed me, I never ceased to be a student, but neither then nor in my days of full-time teaching and studying had I been willing to ask the most searching questions of the moral and political principles on which my sense of myself depended. Whatever threatened or challenged I confined in a safe region of my mind. It was years before I could seriously entertain possibilities contrary to my most deeply rooted opinions. Some mixture of piety and fear kept me from pushing on.

There was no sudden revolution, no burning bush or blinding light, but I caught myself staring out of my office window when I should have been returning phone calls. Fortunate in my circumstances, prosperous, respected, and loved, I found myself strangely restless; answers gave way to questions, and the familiar excitations of daily life faded before the quiet intensity of renewed study. Encouraged by a few friends, I looked again at where I had been and where I was going.

Looking back, I saw that my sense of the world as a reliable place was a useful illusion, but an illusion with a price. I was slow to recognize that all human orders are transient, that all stability is an artful imposition of uncertain duration. The good order of the farm was hardly unique in history, but neither was it the rule, and I whose vision was shaped by it saw, when I looked at the world at large, fair meadows, tranquil villages, and domestic harmony, not cratered fields, smoking ruins, and embittered hearts. For a long time I did not understand that which, in another way, I so clearly knew.

When some of these darker realities advanced from the painted backdrop and assumed three-dimensional form, I felt as if I had gone from the theater to real life. I came to see that the farm, where peaceful people could live and work, was a remarkable achievement of wisdom and will, an island in the ebb and flow of history. I learned to avoid the error of the perfectionists, who expect too much and whose fond hopes turn to rancor when deeds fall short. Measured against dreams, the imperfect justice of man's creations is sadly deficient. Measured against the common operations of our nature over time — lust, laziness, bloodshed, indifference — the higher forms of civil and domestic order are almost radiant.

Radiant, perhaps, but not permanent. I came to see that in this respect the farm, like any secure childhood, was deeply, if properly, misleading. Mother Earth herself grows old, however slowly; much more quickly the fragile institutions of man are transformed or destroyed by the restless agitation of his nature. To me as a boy, every part of the farm was as natural as another, the barn no less than the big rock, the tractor no less than a horse, and the whole a single entity of diverse parts as reliably and naturally there as the earth itself. As a man, I know that in time a farm boy would learn that nature promotes the processes of decay as surely as those of growth, and he would come to understand that only through his skill and attention would machines and buildings remain serviceable or would plants and animals produce. But unless he looked beyond the farm, as some come to do through inclination and accident, he might never see that the farm itself and all the arrangements of the larger realm to which it belonged also depended on human arts. I came to understand that however natural our tendency to draw together, it is only through the cultivation of certain qualities of character that a particular form of association can be created or maintained. The founder, in his rough way, understood it well, as did Grandmother.

Linked by conviction to a supernatural realm yet bound by work and daily habit to the basic rhythms of nature itself, the family united, in a fragile order, aspiration and necessity. Grandmother and my uncles imagined divine love, wisdom, and power even as they dealt with blood and manure, generation and decay. For a while the order held, conferring among its benefits a sense of belonging, significant work, pride of family, ownership, self-discipline, and self-respect. They were uncomfortable with extremes of thought, ambition, or passion. The field on which man's powers and desires were allowed to play was clearly marked and bounded. The farm acknowledged no craving that family bed, table, and bank account could not accommodate, no striving that work and community affairs could not challenge, no seeking that religion, farm management, and casual reading could not satisfy. As I have said, it fostered decency, the middle way.

Over the years the farming community has not only shrunk as fewer farmers have produced more food, it has also drawn closer to the mainstream of American life. It has come full circle, but with an ironic twist. It once thought of itself as the mainstream, later found itself left behind, and then adopted the ways of its urban neighbors. The founder imagined agriculture at the center of the national experience, a case still plausible in his day despite clouds of change on the horizon. He saw a happy fusion of the agricultural way of life, religion and morality, science, republican principles, and political power. For the founder the dominion over the creatures of earth, sea, and air extended naturally to political dominion over a continent. He feared the lure of liberal education, the corruption of slavery, and the call of the West, but they were dangers at the periphery of a self-confident vision. His class, his people, his way of life were at one with the Union.

As the world changed, the farming community had either to change with it or to define itself in increasingly idiosyncratic terms. The little subsistence farms, which produced food to live on and not much to sell, have almost entirely disappeared, and the farms that remain are businesses first and a way of life second. The more ambitious farms were always linked to the economic center — they fed the nation — but they were eventually drawn into the city's moral orbit as well, as rural amusements and ambitions became more closely allied with urban forms. The transformation has been gradual, but with every change in transportation and communication, it has accelerated. The founder saw railroads, canals, and the telegraph help isolated pioneers form farming communities. Grandmother saw improved roads, automobiles, rural mail delivery, daily newspapers, and telephones give farmers ready access to the city. In my lifetime, radio, television, tapes, and videos swept the outside world into the living room in high fidelity and living color.

This much, then, I came to see when I looked back at the road I had traveled. To look critically, however, is in some measure to detach oneself; the independence of the observer, quiet and obedient though he may be, is not the same as the passion of the true believer. But this was not for me a simple change of direction. I was pondering matters of the heart, not opinions only, and I did not want to lose the certitudes that had sustained me. On the route I had come, there was no broad fork clearly marked with highway signs, but the road had diverged, and I had not wanted to follow one path only.

Perhaps I could travel both. And so it was, in another branch of the family, after an old one had died and prayers had been said, the eulogy spoken, that I found myself listening with particular attention to the echoes of old pieties in the swirl of reminiscence and teasing through which the family gave comfort and affection. There in person were bearers of names I had not heard for years, cousins remote and old, my father's friends when young, virtues and peculiarities magnified by time, bodies weakened and diminished. They were more alive in my father's voice than in my meetings with them. Present, too, were their children and their children's children, and I thought I could discern in them shadows of ancient loyalties that might gather substance if the right food were found. I asked myself if these signs could be seeds of new growth or if they were only the traces of a memory which another generation would altogether lose. The way of my ancestors, gone like the great elm, will never come again, but is there a variant strain in which its characteristics, redefined, might yet live?

There lingers still, in some families not long off the farm, a sense of difference, an attachment to family haunts. They imagine that in the past, just before one's time, life was better. Forever quiet now in the photo album are the parents and grandparents — how young they were, how handsome before life marked them, how gentle and devoted in memory. Sentimentality, which colors and obscures all, may be the lie that binds when deeper unity is lost; but lies are shadows of the truth, and in the wistfulness of the heirs I read faint signs of the world I knew as a child.

I felt the sway of the family gods, the old urge to look to the center, drawing a narrow horizon around this little world. I thought that if I were to return, I would come home bearing knowledge of other lands, better able to judge the needs and possibilities of this people. No longer simply or entirely of them, I might see how to revive in modern form the half-forgotten sentiments of another age, how to transform the elements of nostalgia into principles to live by.

The experiment remained untried; sobriety intervened. Comfortable, independent lives do not ask for transformation. There was no oppressor, no land of bondage, no call for Moses. And there were other reasons to hesitate. I once believed that to lead, one must love the people, but later I came to believe that loving is not so simple a thing, not so obvious a good. The romantic and domestic calamities of love are commonplace, eros and prudence being such infrequent companions. So, too, in politics we do not always find an austere, discerning love, free of desire and therefore above the need to flatter. Tears of gratitude when the public applauds say more about the hungry heart of the hero than about his judgment. To lead wisely, then, one must love not the people but the good that is in them or that of which they might be capable. To love the good, one must know it, and to know it, one must know oneself, a dark terrain in which many are lost.

I look back again. For Thanksgiving I would go with my family one year to the farm, the next to my parents' home, to celebrate the holiday with turkey and squash, cranberries and boiled onions, pumpkin, mince, and chocolate pie. For grace there was a poem, a little story, and there were guessing games — how many beans in a bottle or how many pictures could we remember after a walk through a room. We would each sing a song or tell a story. If we were at the farm, we would shoot clay pigeons or try out the black-powder musket Larry had made. In the dining room above the wide oak table, the stamped-tin ceiling bore the dent made by Uncle Sherwin's foot when he was tossed in a blanket as a boy. Under the table was a little shelf where Uncle

Milo kept a box of candies. Uncle Sherwin carved the turkey. Grandmother, Aunt Ellrena, and the other women went back and forth to the kitchen through the big doors the founder had designed so that he could carry bags of wool to the attic. Behind Uncle Sherwin's chair were Grandmother's plants, including the ancient cactus, seeking the pale November sun in the bay window. We thanked the Lord, passed the dishes, praised the food. And we always talked, telling and retelling the family legends. Except for milking, no work was done, but the day was not an interruption of family routine; it was a distillation.

When we celebrated at my parents' house, there was no stamped-tin ceiling, no shooting in the field, but otherwise the day was much the same. Someone would ask again about the brown trout mounted and hung on the dining room wall — twenty-four inches, four and three-quarter pounds, caught in the Black River in Irasburg on a Mepps spinner still hanging from its mouth. I look up as I write. The trout is on my study wall along with photographs that also looked down at us those Thanksgiving days: pictures of my brother and me as boys sitting on some giant blue Hubbard squash my father had grown; of my father and Trixie, the family terrier and the best rat catcher in the neighborhood; of Muggsy the English bulldog, named for the farm's great woodchuck killer; of me with Indian feather, knife, and BB gun; of the 4-H club marching band my father had started; of Uncle Milo holding my brother in his arms. Farm or village, the feast was the same: the same food, the same talk, the same laughter and easy intimacy.

If the broad sweep of family life reflected the spirit of those holidays, so too the life of village, state, and nation reflected, if much less perfectly, some of the characteristics of family. Interwoven with the founding principles of freedom and equality were notions of divine order, love of country, loyalty, self-restraint, and self-reliance; and while even in my childhood, these virtues had come to seem less necessary to the country at large, they had not disappeared. They were fundamental to the farm's understanding of itself, and it was therefore a natural progression to move from the love and responsibilities of the family to the wider community beyond. The good child would become the good citizen, and the boundaries of one's world would be more widely drawn. It would become apparent that just as one had belonged to the family, one belonged, if in a diminished fashion, to the country; brotherhood could be more generously understood. And this was true despite the fact that in some respects farm and family resisted the direction the country was taking and only slowly and incompletely yielded to it.

By such an expansion, home becomes the nation, the nation comprehensively understood not just as founding principle and law but as the environment of custom, habit, loyalty, and affection. Viewed from a certain distance, then, the farm appeared to me not only as a beleaguered remnant of a way of life but as an alma mater whose nurture might prepare its sons and daughters for a wider life and wider service. And so indeed it might; indeed no doubt it has.

Our civil and moral order, to which this wider service would be devoted, is no small accomplishment. At its best it is capable of great decency. Good men and women have worked and died for it, and only by unreasonably exacting standards could one judge that they have worked and died in vain. But for all that, there are wandering spirits it cannot hold, men and women whose imaginations and needs take them to the extremes of thought and conduct. They have, thus considered, an odd similarity, these travelers, seekers, and eccentrics, and when their paths cross, signals sometimes pass. In their various ways, they have felt the limitations of the middle way. They might acknowledge its good-ness, but for them it is not enough; they are reluctant to pay the price. Only the most untamed of them are in the literal sense lawbreakers, but none of them is fundamentally lawful. The best obey out of an independent calculation of the good, not because law moves them as gravity moves water.

Grandmother would have understood the Christian martyrs' defiance of civil law as obedience to a higher order. She did not see moral crises in this country in her time as grave enough to be similarly considered. Lawbreakers were lawbreakers; it was obvious that they should be punished. Because she neither doubted the justice of the law nor questioned the superiority of American political principles, there was no tension in this regard between her innermost thoughts and her public utterance. Life was a journey, but it was not the journey of an exile. Love of home, family duty, political loyalty, and intellectual curiosity coexisted comfortably, indeed coalesced, as do the elements of a painting, in a harmonious design contained by the boundaries of the canvas.

It is unlikely that she thought much, if at all, about those errant spirits whose trajectory takes them beyond the canvas and the frame. If she had, she might have reminded them that no life, not even the life of the freest possible thought, is possible without community. She could have added that we take our preliminary shape in our mother's womb, we learn to speak and walk with the help of our elders, and we are taught by them the rudiments of intellectual, moral, and social discipline. If we are lucky in our nurture, our native powers achieve highly differentiated, effective forms, and we become that which it was in us to be. We are born again into the adult world of family, tribe, church, or state, formalizing with varying degrees of ceremony our incorporation into the larger body. Noble lives are lived within these nourishing confines, and those who would undermine the foundations of such an establishment risk, at the very least, the introduction of less tutored forms.

The profoundest revolutions of thought are accomplished

quietly in the minds and words of the few. Around them gather those with a taste for inquiry and reflection. Some, deeply engaged, will find an intense pleasure quite different from that of the decent middle way; stretching their powers to the utmost, they will pursue their quest to whatever heights it may lead them. If they have ever been at home in the world, however, at one with family and community, they will know, even in their exaltation, that there are no choices without consequences. And no matter what glorious alternatives they encounter or imagine, if they recall with gratitude what they have received from those whose earthbound labor and devotion allowed them to soar, they will speak with reserve and circumspection.

In this old farmhouse in my hilltop village, I have long made what the world calls home. From my study, through the branches of the maple trees, I can see the church on the common. Beyond are the town office building and the old school, now restored for the historical society. To the right of the town offices are the fire pond and the firehouse. The school bus stops by the church. On an October Sunday I hear the church bell ring; it does not ring for me. Later I see my neighbors walking home from church. Father, mother, three sons, a daughter, they stroll through the red and yellow leaves, pause to inspect the remains of the garden, look up at the half-bare trees.

Choices are made. There is always a price.

August 5, 1992

It is forty-eight years to the day since Billy came down with his pony, and we put up the hay machines and ate watermelon. I visit the farm.

I enter the house, now vinyl-clad, and in the kitchen sit with Uncle Sherwin and Aunt Ellrena at a table where the woodstove and woodbox used to be. Aunt Ellrena is in a wheelchair, her mind and body racked by illness; she will die before the year is out. Uncle Sherwin makes her as comfortable as possible, prepares lunch, tries to bring her mind back from its compulsive wandering. At a small worktable in the corner of the kitchen, he makes reproductions of old wooden toys. Uncle Sherwin's son, Larry, and Larry's son, Paul, come in from the shop and field, and they talk about the sweet corn. A few months later at this same table, the men will gather to order vegetable seeds for the following season. It is a good business, fortunate in its location near the city and kept strong by the prudence and industry of three generations. In the fall a pile of two thousand pumpkins will appear in a picture in the local paper. I ask questions, and Uncle Sherwin recalls with perfect clarity a multitude of details about the farm a half century ago, details I have forgotten or never knew.

I go to the front door and walk the length of the house, into the barn ell, and on to the old horse barn where the vegetables are now sold. The distance from the front door of the house to the south wall of the horse barn is about 165 feet. Along the way I see the curly-maple desk and the family photographs in the parlor. There is a television set in the living room, where Grandmother did her needlework in the evenings. Standing in the dining-room bay, once filled with her plants, I look at the dent in the tin ceiling, then at the double row of colored glass in the big window, little squares of yellow, green, rose, red, and blue. I had forgotten the wainscoting of beaded sheathing. The cupboard where the jack-in-the-box lived has exchanged its solid board doors for glass.

I had never examined the shelf clock on the butler's desk which the founder's wife bought from a peddler in the founder's absence and to his great displeasure. On the glass door of the clock, there is a picture of a lady with a yellow dress and bonnet, puffed sleeves, pinched waist, white gloves, brown ribbons, and reddish brown hair, an image of unproductive femininity utterly alien to the realities of farm life but perhaps speaking to some unrecognized longing in the founder's wife. Written in pencil on the back of the glass is the date "Sept 1837," so the clock was bought within a year or two of the purchase of the farm. The maker's paper label is still attached: "Patented Clocks Made and Sold By Northrop & Smith North-Goshen, Conn." Its wooden works still run.

The tin bathtub has disappeared, along with the kitchen's soapstone sink and rocking chair. The storeroom is still a storeroom, filled with baskets, boxes, tools, but now housing snowmobiles and three-wheeled all-terrain vehicles as well. Passing through the car bays and the shop, I climb to the loft, now the museum, where I find samples of barbed wire, photographs, hayforks, crosscut saws, ice saws, hay saws, and a host of other old tools and machines. On the walls of the shop hang more old tools, including the cradle scythe that was passed down in the family and said to be the very one used by the founder the day he broke his health in a burst of intemperance, showing the lazy hired men how the job should be done.

From the door of the shop I look across the lawn where the great elm once stood. Beyond is the road and then the cow barn with its sagging roof. I turn east and then north behind the shop where the pigpens were. The old corn barn and henhouse are gone, lost in the flood. A new henhouse was built and later converted to a modern sugarhouse with an oil-fired evaporator. No more sparks on the night wind. Turning west toward the road, I pass the field from which Grandmother carved her flower garden, an island of beauty, beyond profit and loss, amid the corn and hay.

Across the road at the hay barn, I pause to read a date and the initials of my great-grandfather, William Henry Lester, marked in nails on the big door: "W H L 1882." Above I see in white cutout wood letters the words "Williams Farmstead." In the course of a long reign, Uncle Sherwin renamed the dynasty. A few years after Uncle Milo Lester died, Grandmother wrote, "And so after a hundred years, grandfather Lester's place has changed names. I imagine it will be a good many years before it will be known by any other name than the Lester Farm."

Inside I climb a pile of bales to the great upper beams that span the loft. Knees trembling, I walk across. Below is a concrete floor where once a wood plank could be raised to let the cow's blood drain away during slaughter.

As a boy I simply moved and played and worked here. Now I count things and pace off dimensions. The hay barn is eighty feet long by fifty-two wide, the stable ninety by thirty-two. The stable has about fifty stanchions in two rows with a four-foot walkway behind them and a nine-foot feeding alley between.

The milk cows were sold in 1965, the barn has lost much of its use, and I see decay beyond economic repair. Foundation, roof, and rafter give way as nature reclaims what man so artfully assembled.

The blue Surge vacuum pump is still on the shelf with its logo of orange, blue, and white. Also still in place is the manure bucket's iron track on which I used to chin myself. The stable is mainly a storeroom now — egg cartons, old windows, wire, a motorcycle — but three young Holstein bulls are tied up, soon to be dehorned and castrated; and in the oak pen where the Jersey bull once pawed and snorted, a few chickens peck and scratch.

In the barnyard three steers come to a broken stable window; skittish but curious, they push their pink black-spotted noses toward me and lick my hand. Like the barn cats of my boyhood, they live in a bounded universe largely of man's contriving, and by some dark process of bovine intellection they domesticate, make natural, this intruder.

Tim Perry, the business partner, unloads something from a pickup and puts it in the storage space where the manure spreader once parked, waiting for the day's load. Paul goes by on a three-wheeler, carrying corn from the field to the shop. It is a cloudless day; I leave the barns to walk the land in the August sun.

At the concrete bridge over the river, the south boundary of the property, I look in vain for the pool where I learned to swim. The shifting currents of fifty years have filled it in. East along the river I come to the places where, with Grandmother, I saw the mink and kingfisher. Farther east is the old swimming hole, smaller and less mysterious than in memory but a swimming hole nevertheless, the water dark, the flat rock hot in the sun.

The land stretches farther back than I remembered, but eventually I come to the small brook marking the east boundary. From there it is a short walk to the sugar woods, many of the big old trees still standing, surrounded by a dense undergrowth of little maples. From the highest point of land I look down the valley to the east. The farm my father wanted to buy spreads out below me, the date 1881 marked on the barn roof in slate of contrasting colors.

At the west side of the woods, halfway down the hill, I find the remains of the sugarhouse, the walls gone, the roof rotting into the ground. I leave the woods for the big rock meadow and climb the ten-foot outcropping where I had eaten my lunch Sunday, July 9, 1944. I look west across the fields of vegetables — I can see asparagus stalks and corn, no cows now — to the house and barn and the road, which brings customers from the city. A Ryder truck goes by, an auto carrier, a hundred cars. The barn's dilapidation is obscured by distance. Beyond the barn lies another field, and then the hill on what used to be Uncle Henry's farm, new houses and driveways visible all along the ridge. Beyond the road and south of the creek, I can see the land that once belonged to Uncle Bub, now the site of an auto dealership and a telephone company building. The three farms were contiguous. When the other two sold, they went to strangers, the remaining farm not buying them (as might have seemed wise to do), perhaps following the founder's advice, if not his practice, that instead of "adding more broad acres to his care," the Vermont farmer should manage better what he already owns.

Walking west now, I look in vain for the hemlock spring which I know still exists, although the tree marking it is gone. Next summer Uncle Sherwin plans to clean it out, rebuild the stone walls around the pool, replace the enameled ladle. I will join him; our backs have not bent in common labor for forty years. A Winston cigarette sign, full of bullet holes, leans against the fence. I cross the field along the north line, the unnatural boundary of the founder's making when at his death he divided the original farm between his sons, past the spot where the neighbor cut the fence to let the cows escape the flood, past the ranch house Larry built and lives in, across the road and the next field to where the neighbor's cedar swamp begins.

A deer path comes out of the tall grass at the edge of the field and crosses the brook into the swamp. I kneel and look into the water, a giant above a little world. Water bugs, antennae erect, jerking their legs against the current, ride the surface tension of the pool and cast their shadows on the smooth silt bottom. Fifty years ago the brook never failed; now in dry years it is a trail of mud.

A culvert has replaced the wooden bridge. I cross the brook, walk to the west line of the property, make my way through a dense thicket to the south boundary, which soon joins the river. Not far and I come back to the concrete bridge and the fenced lane by which the cows passed between barn and pasture. It is full of tall grass.

In a few minutes I am back at the house and beyond to the last buildings, a crib for popcorn and the pig barn. At one end of the barn stands the slaughterhouse, quiet now but with echoes for my ears. In the corner is the hearth and overhead the hook and track for carrying the carcass to the boiling water, but the pigpens are gone. In the main part of the barn, used for storage and machine shop, I find the John Deere tractor I drove forty years ago.

Among the odds and ends of the decades is a sign from the community chapel.

AFFILIATED WITH
AMERICAN SUNDAY SCHOOL UNION
REACHING RURAL AMERICA FOR CHRIST
MILL VILLAGE UNION SUNDAY SCHOOL

Ten years ago the chapel gave up its Sunday school and its annual Thanksgiving service with a minister from the city, but neighbors still gather for monthly suppers. This is the evening and, as I say goodbye, someone brings meals for Uncle Sherwin and Aunt Ellrena.

These things pass: the separate world, the divine mission. These endure: love, friendship, work, the land, a neighbor's helping hand. These lie in darkness: the fate of the republic, the shape of souls to come.

Witnesses

❧

The most explicit testimony issues from the words, but the physical papers themselves bear witness, too. The mere fact of their preservation in the scrapbook archives, the care with which the folded papers are opened and passed around for inspection at family gatherings — these signify. And so, like a curator of ancient texts, I listen to the accidents of paper, ink, and sealing wax. Speaking most clearly and in several voices is the diary; serving other uses, it belonged to the family before it came to me.

Although appearing last in this volume, these documents precede the rest of the text in time and might lay claim to other kinds of priority as well. It is in them that I found the roughhewn shape of a way of life, which I have tried to delineate more fully. And it is through them that I glimpsed the antecedents and first steps of a journey that is not yet over.

I have regularized the spelling, verb forms, punctuation, and capitalization of all documents except the diary. Obviously missing or conjectural words appear in brackets. The diary and excerpts from it are printed to represent as closely as possible the appearance in the original.

Man Made for Agriculture
1853

(HENRY LESTER, THE FOUNDER)

The essay appears in a booklet of three sheets of pale blue, faintly lined paper, 9⅝ by 15½ inches, folded once to make six sheets, or twelve pages 7¾ inches wide by 9⅝ inches high. Two large stitches of white thread hold the sheets together, a homemade book of the simplest type, carefully preserved in the family papers but showing a few stains and slightly frayed edges. The founder wrote a small, even hand, rather elegant at first glance, but with many loosely formed letters, which make some words hard to decipher. The faint black letters, some brownish where the paper has begun to brown, march from an even left margin all the way to the right edge of the page.

The founder's spelling is occasionally unorthodox. Fond of rolling, periodic sentences in the fashionable rhetoric of his day, he sometimes wanders asyntactically, but his meaning is usually clear and his expression vigorous, if conventional. No friend of the full stop, he usually marks the end of sentences with a comma or lets them conclude unaided. Commas appear elsewhere in no discernible pattern.

The front of the cover page is blank, but the reverse has the following: "Premium Essay, awarded a premium of five dollars by the Rutland County Society at their fair held at Poultney Sept 1853." The title, "Man Made for

Agriculture," appears at the top of the next page, and in the upper right corner the number 1. The remaining pages are numbered, and the essay concludes on 10, the last page, with the founder's signature.

There was nothing hesitant or subtle about his religious vision. He saw the journey of mankind as a divinely appointed mission from a corrupt Europe to an untamed wilderness in the New World. Here a blend of biblical religion, republican politics, and scientific agriculture would create a prosperous civilization of free men and women. For the founder, the central figure was not Jesus the Redeemer but the creating God, the arbiter of battles, and after Him, on earth, not the fearful sinner or the seeker, but a confident free man, the conquering, independent "agriculturist."

I imagine lines of force descending like a thinning genetic code from the founder through Grandmother to myself, a small boy, and then, further attenuated, to the traveler I have become.

⋙⋘

When the great architect of the universe had created heaven and earth and made light and divided it from darkness, he separated the land from the water, he caused the land to bring forth fruit, the herb-yielding seed and grass, he put lights in the firmament of heaven that should be signs for seasons, for days, and for years, he put the stars in the firmament also and the two great lights, the greater to rule the day and the lesser the night. He created the fish which swim in the sea, the beasts that live upon the earth, the fowls that fly in the air, and every thing that creepeth on the earth. He next created man in his own image, male and female created he them, and gave them dominion over the earth, the sea, the fishes, the beasts, the birds, the herb-yielding seed, and the fruit-bearing tree. He created all things for man and saw that his works were good, and this ended the sixth day. On the seventh day he rested from his labor and sanctified the day as a day of rest. Soon after, our first parents were placed in the Garden of Eden, where was everything desirable for their use (to cultivate the garden) with but one prohibition, that they should not eat of the tree of knowledge; but the subtlety of the serpent and the beauty of the fruit was too much for a person of Mother Eve's construction. She ate and persuaded the man to do likewise, and for this transgression of our first parents, they were sentenced to be agriculturists, in the sweat of their face to eat their bread. The ground was accursed and to ever produce thorn and thistles, and it was only by manual and severe labor that the earth would bring forth bountiful the necessaries of life.

By the foregoing, we see that the supreme being made the earth for the use of man: the beast, the bird, and fishes, the root herb and flowers, the cereal grains and the fruit-bearing trees, the vast ocean, the numberless seas, the mighty rivers and the thousand gentle murmuring rills, the dark heavy forests of timber, and the vast horizon-bound prairies, the pestilence-breeding swamps, the deserts of sand, soils adapted to cultivation or only suitable for grazing. For man was the land divided from the water and made with its surface so various, from the level of the ocean upward to six miles in height, and the climate from the greatest degrees endurable, from heat to cold. The unevenness of the earth was necessary to be useful to man and beast, for herb and flower, for without slight elevations we should not have the abundance of springs which make the murmuring and meandering water rills that, united, make the dancing brooks, then coursing streams and rivers that water the earth and make it fruitful. Without the lofty and rugged mountains that pierce the clouds and whose tops are covered with eternal snow, we could not have the navigable rivers and majestic rivers that are highways for communication for the nations, for commerce, for the exchange of the productions of the earth. Again the unevenness of much of the earth's surface is necessary for pure and healthful air, for grand and sublime scenery, for the growth of all useful timber, trees, and fruit trees and herbs and grass for man and beast. All these are necessary to make man enjoy himself and prosper and be cheerful, for what solitude is more deep and impressive than the solitude of desert or the prairie? Man was made a social being and for agriculture and those arts connected and necessary thereto belonging. Let him not therefore repine and be unsatisfied with his lot, but cheerfully and industriously submit to act in the sphere for which he was created.

The New England farmer combines in his own person and profession both the agriculturist and shepherd. This is necessary to his convenience, comfort, prosperity, and happiness. This is necessary in northern clime to keep the soil from decritating [?]. Our most useful domestic animals are the horse, the ox, and the sheep. The rearing and keeping of these of the best breeds give pleasant and healthy employment, give food and raiment for our use, enrich the soil, and replenish our pockets.

Agriculture in the early ages of the world was but little understood and must have been very imperfect, and the husbandmen must have been poorly remunerated much so for the want of implements. If we look back but one-half century and see the improvement in this art and the tools then in use, we must be amazed at the great change that has been wrought. The crops of grains in the most civilized and intelligent nations of Europe have been more than doubled. This likewise is the case in our New England and that, too, by the Green Mountain boys. For this increase in production, we may look to the greater intelligence of the present generation, the study of agriculture as science, the study of chemistry, the analyzing of plants showing of what they are composed, of what they extract from the earth for their growth, of analyzing soils to learn their component parts, and learning from this what crop the soil will best produce or produce with profit. By chemistry and practical experience, we learn that different crops absorb different elements from the soil. For this reason we have a rotation of crops more than did our ancestors. Chemistry and experiment have settled the point that [if] the soil has been much exhausted of the element that composes one crop, that it will not grow to be remunerating. The soil may be rich in elements wanted for the growth of another crop and grow vigorously. Again the crops have been increased by making, saving, and applying more judiciously a much larger quantity of animal and vegetable manure, by using mineral manures that are absorbed by plants, marl, much guano, lime, bone dust, etc., by a thorough draining of the soil, and finally by a more deep and thorough cultivation of the soil, using a larger quantity of seed and working the soil to more than double the original depth and with less labor. But we must not forget that much of this increase of agricultural productions is owing to the increase and improvement in agricultural implements. Could you see those in use fifty years ago beside those you see this day, you would exclaim: Is the thing possible, was the husbandman compelled to till the soil with those clumsy, unwieldy, awkward instruments? Surely we are a people of progress, can we improve as much for the next half century. For the plows, the first of agricultural instruments now in use, we may claim as much improvement over the ancient instrument as steam engine for travel can over the farm wagon, and as Robert Fulton made his name great as the inventor of the steam engine, let the name of Joseph Nourse [?] be remembered as benefactor of his race for bringing the plow to its present perfection. Should we [be] called on for a sentiment in favor of agriculture, we could but repeat that often given: Speed the plow.

The business of agriculture is followed by a large majority of the civilized portion of mankind, is the most conducive to health, long life, and happiness. It gives a healthy tone and action to the lungs, the heart expands and beats freely, the blood vessels perform their natural duties, the bone cords and muscles by being constantly in use become developed and strengthened, and these, supported by a due proportion of flesh and fat, makes man in reality the lord of creation. The tables of the statistics of Massachusetts, classing each occupation or profession by themselves and giving the average of the length of life to each, show that the agriculturist outlives [by] a number of years that of any other occupation or profession. To make man long-lived, it is necessary that he should have pure air, pure water, wholesome food used in reasonable quantities, a regular systematic diet and habits, temperance in all things, be cheerful and contented with his occupation, rise early and be industrious, and never complain of his hard lot, his poor occupation. In fine he must not sigh for the fleshpots of Egypt. He must [be] thankful that the supreme being created him and ordained him for an agriculturist, placed him on a goodly soil in a good country, surrounded by a good society of his fellows in genial climate where hill, dale, and mountain forest, the grasses, fruit, and grains make the scenery both desirable and beautiful. Let me again repeat that the agriculturist of New England is of necessity both an agriculturist and shepherd. The occupations are not distinct and separate as in olden times, but united as it were with hymeneal bands, not as man and for better or worse, for richer or for poorer, but for good. But yet it [is] a necessary connection to keep the soil in good condition, increase instead of decreasing its productions, and making it more pleasant and profitable for the tiller of soil, his better half, and his little ones, and all connected with his family. This mixed occupation in our New England bears title and name of farmer, and let the farmer be proud that he belongs to that honorable, useful, healthful, rural, independent profession. Let him inculcate this sentiment into his sons and daughters. Let him educate in this faith and for this purpose. I say educate suitable theoretic and practical, for no class need it more, no class can better appreciate, for they are the true yeomanry. On them rest to will and to do the making and sustaining our laws, moral, legislative, and national, and on their suffrages depend them that govern the states and the nation. Was it not the farmer that braved the perils of the ocean and sought this Western world that they might enjoy political and religious freedom, that conquered by indomitable energy and perseverance the savage beasts, the savage men, the savage wilderness, and the more than savage clime? Was it not the farmer that proclaimed the separation from the parent country, that we were a free and independent people, capable of self-government and the election of our own rulers, the making our own laws the great Magna Charta of which is equality, life, liberty, the pursuit of happiness, and the elective franchise with the right to enjoy religious freedom to worship our creator as seemeth good and right to each individual? I ask, were not stern patriots mostly farmers that, ill provided and worse, for seven long years and on many a bloody field beat and humbled the proud Britons with their mercenary allies? The Europeans fought for the will of a monarch and because fighting was their trade; the Americans fought for liberty in the broadest sense of the word, and it pleased the God of battles to give them finally the victory. Has not the farmer more than all others converted the wilderness into arable, productive farms, covered with waving grain, fruits, flowers, and the grasses that give sustenance to millions of domestic animals that give food and raiment and serve for domestic labor and for the pleasure of all? Who so much as the farmers have built these roads and canals, those colleges and institutions of learning, those public and private edifices that adorn the country? In fine does not a large majority of taxes for all purposes come from the pocket of the Vermont farmer? Where else on earth can be found so many elegant and commodious dwellings, adorned with trees and flowers and everything to make home desirable, such convenient roads, so many churches and public schools so well supported, where such deep and general devotion to religion, and where else do the morals and intelligence of the community come up to those of the rural districts of our own Vermont? Let not our sons covet the western prairies or the gold of California when a treasure much greater lies near the surface of our soils, which their industry may bring out by judicious cultivation? Let them not forsake the Green Mountain state to get a competence easier in some unknown clime or untried occupation, for we have horses and sheep superior to any on earth, the rearing of which is sure to lead to competence and wealth. Our cattle too and other domestic animals are but a little behind the best of any lands and richly they reward those who richly feed. Let the Vermont farmer bear in mind that our best animals pay more than double for their keeping than the poorest, that the greatest crops of grain and grass triple the profits of the poorest, that he who stints his soils or his animals must be double-stinted in return, but he who thoroughly manures and cultivates his crops, keeps good stock, and feeds well must reap a rich reward. Let me now offer my opinion that a great perplexity to the Vermont farmer is he has too much land, that instead of buying out his neighbor and adding more broad acres to his care, he should spend his time and money to better manage what he before possessed, that instead of purchasing poor stock because it cost but little, generally the highest price would be the cheapest in the end, that the produce of Rutland County should be doubled, that most farmers would make [less] by doubling their present laboring force [than] by doubling their stocks of manure, by deeper and more thorough cultivation, by better and more durable fencing their land, and by keeping better stock and giving better feed. Young men and maidens, agriculture is your most safe employment, the most sure of competence, long life, and happiness. But few fail that pursue this with alacrity, when in the mercantile and other professions, but few are prospered, and those few mostly, whether statesmen, jurists, or merchant princes, retire at last to agriculture that their last days be serene and happy. Again, agriculture not only being the most useful, healthful, and independent occupation, tends more than any other to lead the mind to religion, morality, and virtue, and make man feel and act towards his fellow man like the good Samaritan, and how few educated in the rural districts in schools and high schools, and learn and follow the agricultural profession through their minority, fall into vicious habits and are [a] curse to themselves and community thereafter. A man's education must not be measured by the years of common school attendance, the length of his academic course, or the size of his college diploma. The two first are useful when young to give him an introduction to a habit, a desire to learn in his leisure moments that may grow with his growth and strengthen with his strength until in mature years he will be found to possess much useful knowledge. It is folly to suppose that a few years at our institutions of learning alone will make a man deeply read. The collegiate course is almost sure to spoil a man for an agriculturist, a merchant, any useful mechanical trade or profession that requires manual labor. Six years of youth spent, and one-half that is studied that will never be in the least beneficial or practical for use. In these six years, he has contracted the habit of idleness, of a superiority to others not pursuing the same course, and practically reversing the order laid down by the God of nature who said the day was made for labor, the night for repose. The collegian with AB then says his education, whether he has acquired much or next to nothing, must give him a living, is averse to anything like labor except it be the labor of writing and teaching. He of course takes to teaching divinity or law, and these professions are overcrowded or the collegian lacks the ability to fill these stations successfully, and a majority fall back on connections or community, an incubus, a dead weight and drone, setting at nought the decree of his creator that in the sweat of his brow should he eat bread. Liberally educated men are necessary for teachers, jurists, and divines, but aversion to manual labor or an intellect below mediocrity in youth are sound reasons why he should not go through the collegiate course. Further, the agriculturist, raising most things for their own use and for the support of all, is the most independent class. They have the creator's promise that seedtime and harvest shall not fail. They are the grand conservators of freedom and democracy throughout the world. On their will rests the continuance of this republic. They might dictate by their suffrages who should be legislators in every state in the union. Besides their numerical strength, no occupation is more honorable. In the republics of Rome and America, they have filled the highest offices in the civil and military and been crowned with laurel as heroes, patriots, and statesmen. Should this republic be destined as was Rome to fall to pieces by its great distention, or some successful military chieftain seize on and subvert the government, or should absolutism tread out democracy with its iron heel in the Old World, and hurl her millions of cossacks on our shores and threaten to wipe republicanism from the earth, then may the eagle of liberty find a safe resting place in the fastnesses of the Green and White Mountains and true patriots a rallying point over the graves of Allen, Warner, Stark, and their compatriots, and from thence advance until despotism and monarchy be wiped off the face of the earth, and universal liberty and democracy be established, or until the lion and lamb lie down together for all time.

On Horses and Horsemen
c. 1862

(EXCERPTS FROM HENRY LESTER'S

ESSAY ON HORSES)

Lacking a title (I gave it the title shown), a signature, or any other identifying mark, but clearly in the founder's hand and style, the essay is written in black ink on five sheets of slightly yellowed, white, lined paper, 7⅞ by 9⅞ inches. The sheets are numbered at upper left, front and back, one through nine, with the text ending at the bottom of nine.

A few excerpts are reproduced here. Written during the Civil War, as an internal reference makes clear, the essay is later than "Man Made for Agriculture" and more irascible in tone, perhaps reflecting ill health (the founder was to die December 3, 1864) or simply an aspect of his disposition. According to Grandmother, he was sometimes "cantankerous and ornery."

[Horses are more expensive and troublesome to keep than other domestic animals] . . . therefore the least number we keep comparatively to our business as agriculturists the better, as other stock will better replenish the purse, which is a great and necessary aim of the Yankee farmer.

•

The greatest curse that ever befell this republic next to the present civil war is the mania for horse racing and fast trotting. Perhaps the expense to individuals and community for 60 years past will exceed that of the war since its commencement. Besides encouraging, aiding, and abetting the worst and most injurious vices, the fast horse man is with scarce an exception [a] gambler and tippler, a boon companion with the black leg, a frequenter of brothels, a spendthrift of his time and means, generally comes to his end prematurely and in poverty, dies a disgrace to manhood, and falsifies the commands of his creator that by the sweat of his brow [he] should eat his bread.

•

Such horses as I have spoken of are mere sporting animals and to the farmer are worse than useless. Put them to usual business that we want horses to perform and their sporting qualities are destroyed. I next allude to the cruelty to the animal. This racing and fast trotting, all the power and cunning of subtle man, aided by the more subtle Devil, is employed by whipping, spurring, and shouting to get the utmost speed out of the horse. Many have broken down under this vile and wicked treatment and died soon after, even in the short race. For the long race many have trotted their 20 miles in less than an hour, and many have died unable to perform this feat, and all this to gratify the passion of sporting man in this so called Christian nation, and no laws on our statutes to punish these miscreants. To find a fast-horse man that was a good farm manager or even [?   ] as an agriculturist is or would be like hunting for a white blackboard or a black weasel.

The present war, horse running, and Negro slavery are one

[and] all Southern institutions, all detestable to the true lover of God and his country . . .

•

In breeding horses as well as other animals, like are apt to beget and bear their like.

•

The colt, like all other domestic animals, must be kept well the first year. Otherwise and after, all the best care, feed, and attention will not make them outgrow this year of neglect, and the balance sheet for raising will outfigure the worth of the animal. For your summer pasture for colts, you should have high, rough, rocky ground. By this the colts will become more muscular by moving about their limbs, more pliable and surefooted. Habits acquired when young by horse or man are not often forgotten when mature. Train up a child when young in the way he should go, and when he is old he will not depart from it, said a wise man of olden time. The same is true of a colt. Train young, train calmly, moderately, firmly. Next, your fence to the colt pasture should be at least five and a half feet high, firm and substantial, for if your colt has the spirit and bottom that he ought to have, leaping fences and going where he pleases and circulating about generally and getting in company with other colts is very easily learned and never forgotten.

•

The third winter is the proper time to break the colt to the saddle and harness. Teach him as you would a child, easy lesson first. When he understands it, give him another, then a recess. The next time make him repeat his former lessons, then give a new one, and so on, lesson after lesson. You progress in this way and soon the colt has a pride in carrying you in harness. A horse is an animal that will soon become much attracted to man if they are kindly used. They possess much [more] intelligence than they are given credit for, and although they never can speak any human dialect, they soon learn what is said to them and understand it. Always call your horse by a name. He will then know he is meant when others are present. By the same means, he [knows] to start, go fast or slow, and stop at your bidding. No whip or whipping is needed to a well-brought-up horse. The whip is a relic of barbarism. Let it be discarded, or if you have a good one, drive to town, hitch up, and leave it in your wagon. Someone that needs it more will soon possess it. Gone, well, don't fret and hunt about for it. You are better without it. Or will you carry your whip about town in your hand or under your arm as some do? When I see this, I always think of a slave driver, lashing human flesh and blood for wages. He might be some degenerate son of the North that has emigrated to a more balmy clime and forgotten or left behind those early precepts he should have received. The early training of the horse has much to do [to] make his future character and usefulness. His disposition will assimilate to that of his breaker. He will be kind, gentle, and true, and obedient to perform his task, or fractious, ugly, balky, sulky, and tricky.

A Dying Man's Letter to His Son
1856

(MOSES LESTER,

THE FOUNDER'S FATHER)

The paper is a single sheet, white, lined, 7¾ by 12⅜ inches, written on one side only and folded to make a mailable letter, 2¹¹⁄₁₆ by 4⁷⁄₁₆ inches, addressed to Mr. H. W. Lester, Rutland, with no stamp but with traces of orange (originally red?) sealing wax. I notice some yellowing of the paper, several brown stains, some tearing along the fold lines. I wonder if the brown ink was once black. At top center is the date, Feb.y 25th 1856; the signature, Moses Lester, is at lower right, and the name of the son appears at lower left.

The author apparently considered himself a dying man (the title is mine) with advice to give while he was still able. If the letter is any indication, he was a gentler man than his son, more respectful of book learning, worried that his daughter-in-law might harm herself through overwork. He lived almost two years more, dying on November 23, 1857.

Rutland Feb.y 25th 1856

Dear Son, I would have said a few words more to you the other day, but I am so deaf it was not convenient. My health is very poor, and I have so many infirmities about me I must soon be gone. It is wonderful I have been spared so long, I hope for a wise purpose. God knows best; I wait his time. In my reflecting hours, I think much of your dear family. You and your dear respectable wife have been laborious, and it seems to me you have abundance, and I should be pleased to see you enjoy it. Superintend and hire others to do the work without and within, keep a good hired girl or two, and let your wife direct; [it] will be enough for her. She is ambitious and will soon fail, I fear. Your only daughter, Mary, has never had but little opportunity to learn in our small schools. Send her to Castleton. There are good families where they will take good care of her and feel interested in her education. Now is the time to improve it. Times have altered and you must keep up with the times if you want your family respected and noticed. I think you will never regret it. What can you do better with property than all is necessary on your family. See those who seem to have but little means send their children abroad to learn. Gilbert is a fine boy; give him a good common education at least. If you think you can't spare him in the summers, send him to some academy abroad in the winters and don't confine him to work too much and too hard. W. H. I want you to keep at school, and don't think our a. b. c. schools will do for him. He must have an education. Let us have one Lester in our family who has an education; it won't hurt him for a farmer. He may be a great man and possibly a bishop. Strive to keep up the dignity of our name in our families. If we do not, we may not expect others will. Much depends on the education of children to make them respectable. I have named these few thoughts as they occurred to my mind. Your judgment will better direct your own concerns. I feel interested in your welfare and keep my mind busy on something. If you think I have said too much, excuse me. My health is failing daily, and your health now is no security against death. Let us be prepared for the solemn hour is the fervent prayer of your affectionate father.

Moses Lester

As I Remember
c. 1955

(PAULINE WILLIAMS,

THE GRANDMOTHER)

Grandmother's reminiscences occupy twelve pages of a family scrapbook; the last page is a separate section, entitled "Echoes of the Flood." The sheets are heavy scrapbook stock, buff-colored, 9 by 10⅝ inches, yellowed around the edges, unnumbered, undated, but initialed at the end of the main section. The thick-lined, blue-green script (a wax pencil?) is plain and clear, reflecting the character of the author. To judge from certain internal evidence and from other items in the scrapbook, the reminiscences were probably written in the early or mid-1950s, well before her death on September 25, 1962.

Grandmother's nostalgia, affection for the farm, and respect for her family are plain to see. There are hints, too, that she shared the founder's robust faith, his blend of piety and worldly endeavor, but she judged less harshly than her stern progenitor and saw more clearly the need for a salvation not of this world.

Out of the long ago I can see my grandmother Lester contentedly knitting in the little old Windsor rocking chair. As one watched her, you could plainly see pictured in her face the memories she cherished, her honor and integrity, her self-respect and conscience. In all these things she was a rich woman.

As a little girl I remember sitting at her knee peering up under her gold bowed glasses to make her laugh.

Then she would lay aside her knitting and tell me some stories. Perhaps it would be about Little David and Great Goliath, with a tiny, wee voice for Little David, and a great, heavy voice for Great Goliath. Perhaps it might be about Noah and the Ark, when it rained forty days and forty nights, or again about Elisha and the bears. I think perhaps this was told for the moral it contained.

Of the time when she lived on Lester Meadows in Chittenden, and hearing the frightening call of the panthers, sounding like babies crying in the woods. Bears, too, were very plentiful, seeing them very often when they went for the cows, and one as bold as to visit the pigpen and carry one home for its supper. Owls with their eerie notes calling each other, making chills run up and down your spine, with their who-ooo-oo-ing. And the time when her first baby came, all alone save a young girl to help her through the first great experience of her family life.

As I close my eyes I can seem to hear Grandma saying, "Where in canopy are my glasses?" and after looking awhile for them, find them pushed up on her forehead. Also, looking out of the window, perhaps she would say, "Why it's as dark as a pocket. Where in tunket has the time gone to?" And even today, I hear very clearly out of the past Grandma's wise admonition "Waste not, want not." I can say with all truthfulness that I have tried to live up to this wise saying. If perchance I should have to go over the hill to the poorhouse, it will be with a clear conscience.

And so Grandfather and Grandmother Lester, having decided they would go to Rutland to live, left their home in the wilderness of Chittenden, where they lived ten miles from any neighbor on land that is now flooded by waters of the Chittenden Dam. They bought this farm of a man named Hodges. It is located on the Pittsford Road about three miles north of Rutland City, or Village, as it was then called. The village at that time comprised only a few buildings on North Main Street.

This place of about two hundred acres was later divided between Grandfather's two sons, my father and Uncle Gilbert, my father keeping the home place of about eighty-two acres.

They lived in a little old house just a few feet south of the present one. When the new house was built, a plank was laid from the old house to the new, so [one] could walk from one to the other.

Often one remarks about the big doors in the house, so made to give plenty of room to carry huge bags of wool to the attic, after shearing the sheep. I have heard my father say a carpenter was all winter making the doors.

Judging from what our forebears have told and from what you gather from looking at his picture, Grandfather Lester was a very stern and unyielding sort of a man.

He was an excellent farmer, prosperous and well known for his stock: cattle, horses, and sheep. He was interested in agriculture advancement, and had much to do with starting what we call fairs. At that time there would be a one-day showing of stock, usually on some street in Rutland or nearby towns.

He was well read, and as my father used to tell, he would sit by the fireplace, candle in one hand, tallow dripping down, paper in the other, rapt in the latest news, or studying some farm paper. At one time he wrote a thesis on agriculture, receiving a prize of $5.00 for the paper.

But Grandfather had his troubles, especially with farm help.

At that time help was very cheap; often board and tobacco would pay them, and, I suppose, cider thrown in. One day Grandfather had to go away, and gave instructions to the men to do some cradling while he was gone. [To cradle was to cut grain with a cradle scythe, which laid it out evenly.] Evidently the men fell down on their job, for when Grandfather came back and found the men had shirked, he was so furious he grabbed the cradle and showed them how work should be done. That was one time his sound judgment and common sense failed him. Anger and over-work were too much, since that was the last hard work he ever did, and he died not long after, a man in his fifties.

I like to think of him as an exceptionally smart man, shrewd as an old Yankee should be. How he got Mr. Hodges out of bed at midnight to make the last payment on this place, Grandfather having the money ready and anxious to pay before the date set, probably to save a little interest. So at the stroke of twelve o'clock midnight, the final payment was made on the day it was due, and I suppose a great deal of satisfaction on Grandfather's part.

And so, my grandfather Lester, all honor due for the good deeds you did. If sometimes you were cantankerous and ornery, it will be veiled with understanding, knowing we all have our shortcomings and difficult times in life the same as you. For the seed you left, all thanks be given.

Grandma lived a great many years after her husband's death, patiently waiting, knitting, ever knitting, until the time came for her to put it aside, and go into the great beyond. My grandparents are buried in the family lot in Evergreen Cemetery. He erected the monument before he died.

It is my earnest wish that in the years to come, there will be someone to put fresh flowers on the lot, some time throughout the years, in loving memory of those who have passed through the Western Gate.

I miss seeing the old barn that Grandfather used to keep his young cattle in. It was just north of the sugar woods over the stone wall. They used to ride horseback to feed them, and drive them to the brook for water. It was torn down long ago. And another old landmark has disappeared.

The old sheep barn on the flat we used to call the flat barn, and is used now as a bull barn on Orin Thomas's farm. This flat barn had running water, piped from the hemlock spring, so the sheep could have access to fresh water. How often we used to watch tramps as they started out in the morning, having had shelter in the old barn during the night. How well I remember the beech grove, the trees with their lovely gray bark, smooth and shiny, the three-sided fruit, with the delicious meat inside, and in the fall the leaves with serrated edge turning a beautiful brown.

The old orchard where the big rock still stands sentinel, keeping its secrets of the years past and a landmark we all love. An old rail fence surrounded the orchard, and keeping within its confines a variety of apple trees our grandfather set out.

How well his grandchildren remember sitting on the top rail in the northeastern part eating the luscious Striped Sweets, the August Sweets on the western side, yellow and the melt-in-your-mouth kind. On the south side huge Pound Sweets, with their watery cores, what a noise we made sucking in the juice of their lusciousness.

Northern Spys — never again will there be apples to equal their flavor, especially with popcorn and sweet cider on cold winter evenings, when we gathered around the table in the sitting room with our family and often friends to join in our fun.

Electric lights? O no! A very friendly kerosene hanging lamp added to our cheer. An old Stewart coal-burning stove gave us warmth. Can you imagine the comfort on a cold wintry night, with your shoes off, and several pairs of feet on the skirt around the stove? All toasting their feet and visiting before going upstairs to bed.

What fun the little boys (Walter and Milo) used to have chasing chipmunks along the old rail fence. One would say, O there he goes, but where, we look everywhere, O there he is, clear out on the end of the rail, and surely enough, the cunning little fellow had raced through the hollow rail, to lead another merry chase for the little boys to follow. Up and down the corners, over the ground, and then again through their favorite raceways till both boys and chipmunk are tired out, and seek other pleasures.

I wonder if there are many boys and girls who lived on a farm who can't remember switching apples. We would cut withes from apple trees, gather our blouses or aprons full of small green apples, scramble to the top of the big rock, attach an apple to the end of the switch, reach as far back as we could, and with all the force we had throw it far out into space, if we had good luck. It wasn't always on top of the big rock, anywhere we could pick up a few apples and a switch.

One asks which came first, the hen or the egg, or you might say the oak or the acorn. But anyway when we were young, there was a big oak tree on the western side of the woods just at the edge. One big limb was just low enough so we could reach the end, pull it down, hang on tight, and swing out ever so far, as the limb went up into the air again.

There are so many things come to my mind when I am thinking about times long ago. Lillian setting fire to the closet in Uncle Milo's bedroom. Took in a match to see her pretty new dresses. Anna and Etta taking out their big wax dolls, and taking me out on stoop, cradle and all.

Of the bookcase in parlor that used to be a cupboard, and when Grandma did her baking in the brick oven, she would make a number of mince pies, freeze them, and store in this cupboard (talk about freeze lockers). At that time there was only a small door between the living rooms, so could be shut tight in the winter.

Talk about the good old days, or were they when one stops to think about shearing sheep for wool to be spun and made into cloth, also flax to be made into linen, and then made into clothes and household linens. When you see the tailor's goose, think of the men's and boys' clothing that was made at home. The wooden shoe lasts the cobbler used when he came to make shoes. The tallow candles, soft soap, and you made your own lye. I did not like soft soap to wash dishes, but I remember what a lot of suds it made (an old-fashioned detergent).

When Sunday morning came Dad would try to round us all up to go to church, and what a job he had. Best shoes would pinch, stockings wouldn't match, neckties not to be found, hair wasn't cut, or something was the matter, to make getting ready for church a terrible ordeal. If enough were going to fill the surrey, out would come the horses to be hitched on, and off we would go. Congregational Church in Rutland. My grandfather bought a pew at one time, and I like to think of it as the home pew.

After dinner sometimes we would go walking up in the woods with Dad or perhaps he would take us all to ride. In the evening we would gather around the piano, and sing old familiar songs. Dear old Dad, what a job he must have had bringing us seven children up without a mother. My mother died when I was about five years old. About all I can remember of my mother was the day when all the folks were away and there was no dinner to get, and Mother took Grandma Lester's dinner to her on a tray. On this tray, so far as I can recall, was a piece of mince pie and cheese. Isn't it queer how such things stay by you for so many years?

My father married again when I was around ten or twelve years old. My stepmother was kind to me and the boys.

The years have slipped by. Anna was married, then Etta, and so on down the line except Uncle Milo. It was my privilege to make a home for him, and I think it was a happy one, as he made a happy one for me and my children.

He was the farmer of the family, and I think Grandfather Lester would have approved of his method of farming.

Came June 3, 1947, and all day the river rose higher, till about six o'clock, when the water began to recede. But somehow I did not feel quite sure we should stay in the house that night, so I called Uncle Henry and Mildred, and they were so good as to have us come over for the night.

We started about eight o'clock, and as we were driving out of the yard, a great wall of water came rushing down the river. Ellrena said if she ever offered a fervent prayer it was then, that the car would not stall.

Uncle Milo, Sherwin and Clarence (hired man) were just a bit too late because Clarence had to change his shoes the last minute. The truck stalled, but [the] men got a ride to dry ground.

I will never forget how kind Uncle Henry and Mildred were to keep us till we could get back in the house again. Ellrena was so good to carry on and clean up for me after the flood.

It was a terrible experience, but out of it all you remember the many kind things your folks and friends did for you.

It was a terrible blow to Uncle Milo, so much love, thought, and hard work went into the farm, and so severely damaged in just a few hours. I think he failed gradually from that time till his death.

Etta and Milo are buried in the family lot in Evergreen Cemetery.

And so after a hundred years, Grandfather Lester's place has changed names. I imagine it will be a good many years before it will be known by any other name than the Lester Farm.

Grandfather Lester's great-grandson, Sherwin Lester Wil-

liams, and two great-great-grandsons, Larry and Gareth, will
carry on. God bless you and keep you and make his face to shine
upon you, and be gracious unto you. Now and forever more,
amen.

P.L.W.

ECHOES OF THE FLOOD

Henry Alexander, James Russell, Donald Swan coming early to
help Sherwin clean out the mud. Charles and Charlotte coming
down to help. Charlotte taking clothes, curtains, and things home
to clean, coming down again to put up curtains and bringing food
to eat. Charles digging in mud to find my sterling-silver spoons.
The spoons were on bureau in dining room. Water tipped it over.
Uncle Milo leaning on broad shelf looking out pantry window,
tears running down his face.

Big bull pouts in little pools of water in the meadow.

Charlotte Thomas bringing down a cake one morning, neighbors sending in vegetables to can. Libby Swan cooking our dinner
and sending it over first time we came back to stay from Uncle
Henry's.

How hard it was for us all to keep going, but Sherwin made
it. Uncle Milo always said he was good to assume responsibility.

Diary Book
1944

(CHARLES FISH)

It was fatter once, this stained and battered book, its thinness, when it came to me, a testimony to the frugality of careful people. After other uses, pages were discarded; those remaining were to be my diary. I cannot remember what moved me to record the day's events, some nascent autobiographical impulse or the urging of my grandmother, a maker of scrapbooks and keeper of family memories. Whatever the initial thrust, it must have been Grandmother who found the book, for under her watchful eye nothing was wasted or lost.

Its provenance would not have interested me at the time—I turned eight that summer and was innocent of historical curiosity—but later I discovered that it was originally a record book for the transactions of the farm. About 7½ by 12 inches, covered with tan cloth printed in an ornate design to resemble tooled leather, and bearing the words "Day Book," it has lined pages with seven columns of various widths for recording sales and purchases. The pages are numbered; 81 through 164 survive. They were originally sewn, and as the entire gathering began to pull loose from the cover, someone restitched them in two places with brown yarn.

Useful information is printed inside the front and back covers. On the front cover, from the "Table of Days Between Two Dates: A Table of the Number of Days Between Any Two Days Within Two Years," I find that there are 258 days between June 3, 1892, and February 16, 1893. In the "Weight Per Bushel of Grain, Etc.," I can look up the "number of pounds per bushel required, by the law or custom, in the sale of articles specified in the several States of the Union." The table lists the District of Columbia and thirty-one states, and includes figures for barley, buckwheat, coal, "corn shel'd," corn meal, onions, oats, potatoes, rye, wheat, salt, turnips, "beans wh.," "clover S'd.," and timothy. The "Carrying Capacity of a Freight Car" tells me that a ten-ton car can carry up to sixty barrels of whiskey, fifty to sixty head of hogs, or 200 sacks of flour. "A Short Method for Calculating Interest" says that if I multiply the principal by "as many hundreds as there are days" and, for a four percent loan, divide the result by 90 or, for a twelve percent loan, by 30, I will get the answer. Fifty dollars at four percent for thirty days will earn 16⅔ cents. The table "Quantity of Seed Required to Plant an Acre" lists fifty-four kinds of seeds, including four kinds of clover or clover mixes and six grasses. For cucumbers in hills it takes three quarts, for broadcast peas three bushels.

I am instructed to see the back of the book for "other valuable information" and there I find under "Interest Laws and Statutes of Limitations" that in Vermont six percent is the legal rate and the rate allowed by contract and that the statute of limitations is six years for judgments, notes, and open accounts; whereas in California the legal rate is seven, there is no limit on the contract rate, and the statutes of limitations are five, four, and two. The table lists forty-seven states and territories and the District of Columbia. Under "Domestic Weights and Measures" I note that in apothecaries' weight twenty grains equal one scruple and in mariners' measure 120 fathoms equal one cable length. "Foreign Moneys" tells me that in England four farthings equal one penny and in the Austro-Hungarian Empire 100 kreutzers equal one florin. In the last entry, "Business Law in Daily Use," which "contains the essence of a large amount of legal verbiage,"

I learn that "principals are responsible for the acts of their agents," "ignorance of the law excuses no one," "the Law compels no one to do impossibilities," "contracts made on a Sunday cannot be enforced," and "a contract made with a lunatic is void."

Of the original use of the book two fragments remain, both of which would remind a sentimental observer that one of the purposes of farming was, as the founder said, to "replenish our pockets." They are not in the same hand. The first, a plain script, is probably Grandmother's, while the second, more elegant, may be my great-grandfather's. The first is as follows:

Salt	spices	crackers
Mar 14 curing salt .90	pepper .10	(2) lbs .33
	Sage .15	4½" .81
		4½" .77

Mar 14 oysters .30
2½ Fish .56

And the second:

Supplies

1903			
Apr	2	10 pieces of 12 in. tile @ .80	8 00
"	"	557 ft. plank @ $14.00 per thousand	7 80
"	7	4 blocks marble @ 1.00 each	4 00
"	8	4 pieces of 8 in. tile @ .40	1 60
"	8	4 loads of gravel @ .10 of Russell	40
"	9	1 " " " @ .10 of Davis	10
"	9	3 " " " @ .10 of Mrs. Gillam	30
"	17	F. Provo repairs	1 75
"	16	Hammer 1.15 2 shovels .75 1.50 jack 25	2 90
Oct	19	36 load of gravel @ .10 Mrs. Gillam	3 60

"	20	10	"	"	"	@	.10	Mrs. Gillam			1	00
"	20	13	"	"	"	@	.10	Mr. Pinney			1	30
"	21	59	"	"	"	@	.10	"	"		5	90
"	22	56	"	"	"	@	.10	"	"		5	60
"	24	83	"	"	"	@	.10	"	Pennock		8	30
"	28	16	"	"	"	@	.10	Vt. Marble Co.			1	60
"	29	28	"	"	"	@	.10	Vt. Marble Co.			2	80

" One Plow Point

Nov 4 8 loads crushed stone

" 6 14 " " "

" 18 63 loads of gravel @ .10 per load Edgar Davis   6 30

" 12 91 loads of crushed stone

Nov 4 Fred Provo repairs   2 40

In "The Table of Days Between Two Dates," the years chosen for an illustration are 1892 and 1893, presumably close to the time the book was manufactured and perhaps not long before the family purchased it. The date 1903 in the fragment above is proof of its use by the family in that year. The book is about one hundred years old.

The second use of which there is tangible evidence was to hold stamps. I find Uncle Sherwin's initials "SLW" in blue block letters, irregular and bold, at the bottom of the cover, and at the top the words ''STAMP ALBUM'' in the same hand. Nearer the center of the cover, in smaller, fainter, penciled letters, appear the words ''DIARY BOOK,'' the volume's third and final purpose. The stamps and the pages that bore them are gone; but in addition to the evidence on the cover, "turkey British Honduras New South Wales" appear at the top of one page, "Foreign Stamps" on another, and, in large block letters, the following words scattered on several pages: REVENUE, CANADA, SWEDEN, SWITZERLAND, TURKEY, POLAND, AUSTRALIA, GREECE, BRITISH COLONIES, BELGIUM, COSTA RICA, EGYEPT, FINLAND, JAPAN, ITALY, BERMUDA, and VICTORIA.

Every scrap but one testifies, the curing salt as well as my own daily entries, and in the web of spiritual archaeology they interrelate, however disparate and detached they are in origin. (One entry, in a hand not found elsewhere, makes no sense: "(Honorary   'Esquire'."). For my quest is not historical, or if historical, only by way of transit to the contemporary. And the truly contemporary is the permanent, the enduring, the substratum of human nature and the various arts by which human beings form themselves into moral individuals and purposive communities.

I am surprised at the power of the physical object to move me — the rough tan cover, the traces of other lives, my own careful, if awkward, hand, the attempt at regularity and precision in marking each entry. Despite my care, I marked two entries as "42 th day"; two as "66 th day"; two as "67 th day"; five successive days as "52 th," "51 th," "52 th," "53 th," "53 th"; five successive dates as August 15, August 16, August 15, August 15, August 16; and two as August 18. I dated every entry and skipped no day; I was in earnest.

❧

First day   June 10, 1944

I went down street and got a new pair of tennis shoes and two packages of bbs also two banana-splits. I am down on the farm for the summer. I got my bb-gun and bow and arrows.

Charles

Second Day   June 11, 1944

Today I went to church and got My Bible. I shot two sparrows with my bb-gun. they are the hardest little pest to get a shot at. My father and Mother and My Brother went home today. every day I go out to hunt. I rode down with the milk.

Charles

Third day   June 12, 1944

I went fishing with Dicky Thomas and the Smith boys. they had luck but I did not. they got red fin-salmon and gave me three and I ate them for supper. I went in swimming first time this year.

Charles

4 <u>th</u> day   June 13, 1944

I went fishing and got a minnow. I started sproutind potatos today. My bb-gun is plugged up. I had a card from mother, they got home safely   The Daily Mirror says fair and warmer today but it should say fair and cooler today.

Charles

5 <u>th</u> day   June 14, 1944

The Russell boys came up to play and went swimming and fishing. The Russell boys caught ten fish together. I caught a dce and a red fin-salmon. I am still sprouting my potatoes. I lost my bait box and my pants but found them.

Charles

Charles

My dog is old. He is old and tired. I remember when we had fun together. He is old now. But we still love him. We useto have fun with him. I hope I can have a other dog. they are good for pets. I like them. they are very nice. Someday I will have a other dog. His name will be tom. He is gong to be a collie. I hope he will be nice. love nobody

no part of the Diary

6 <u>th</u> day   June 15, 1944

Grandma and I went fishing. I caught three fish and pulled one out but fell off my hook back into the water and I lost him. We followed the river up to the end of Uncle Milos properity. We saw a kingfisher dive for a fish the first time in my life. finished potatoes today.

Charles

7 <u>th</u> day   June 16, 1944

I went fishing with Clarence we both caught two fish they were red fin-salmon. We had a thunder shower. Harold unplugged my bb-gun and took out thirty-five b-b's.

Charles

8 <u>th</u> day   June 17, 1944

I went down to Moore's sawmill with Uncle Milo after some boards. I went fishing with Dicky Thomas and Bucky smith I caught a red fin-salmon Dicky caught a sucker about a foot long.

Charles

9 <u>th</u> day   June 18, 1944

A prisoner escapes they shot at him on Woodstock Ave. and were looking all over Quirks farm for him. I hope they find him. Grandma and I went to Sunday School today and Audrey gave me a piece to learn for Childrens day.

Charles

10 <u>th</u> day   June 19, 1944

The man who was captured yesterday was a homicidal maniac. they found him north east of Rutland city. I ran out of ammunition for my bb gun. grandma and I had dreams about him.

Charles

11 <u>th</u> day   June 20, 1944

Having a thunder shower now. We took some wood up to perley's house. we ran out of cas and had to walk home. Uncle Sherwin took up some cas but we still had "putwer" and "putwer" with it. Joan Hack came down to play with me.

Charles

12 th day   June 21, 1944

Uncle Sherwin shot a red squirrel out of the elm tree. He blew that little pest all to smithereens. We went up to Mr. Eayres after two hogs. I went up in the corn with Uncle Milo and Clarence.

Charles

13 th day   June 22, 1944

Uncle Milo bought me two packages of bb's. I planted a little garden today with corn pumpkins string beans musk melons and water melons.

Charles

14 th   June 23, 1944

A load of logs went by this afternoon. Just as it went by the horse barn a tire blew out, a piece of the rubber flew in the barn. The driver came in called up the gas station and said his tire "blew all to hot place"   Billy Thomas came down to play with me.

Charles

15 th day   June 24, 1944

Rained nearly all day. I helped Uncle Milo fix the truck today. I milked two cows tonight one was pretty steppy.

Charles

16 <u>th</u> day   June 25, 1944

Childrens day at Chapel today. I recited my piece. It was a good program. The cows got out and ran for the hay meadow, they came like stampede through the gate

Charles

17 <u>th</u> day   June 26, 1944

I ate my last piece of strawberry short cake for the season and O boy was it good! My string beans are coming up. I dyed two feathers today one blue and one red.

Charles

18 <u>th</u> day   June 27, 1944

The men started cutting hay in bridge meadow. It has been very hot today so I went swimming with Larry and aunt Ellrena and Grandma. I receivd five post cards in the mail today.

Charles

19 <u>th</u> day   June 28, 1944

Uncle Milo said he might learn me to drive the hay truck. The men got the first hay today. Uncle Sherwin caught a live young woodchuck today.

Charles

20 <u>th</u> day   June 29, 1944

The woodchuck was not kept in captivity a great while. He wanted to go back to his hole so he decampted. But we think Mugsy caught him and made a meal out of him. We had two thunder showers today

Charles

21 th day   June 30, 1944

Muggsy and I cornered a wood chuck in the stone wall. We had a lot fun trying to get hin out. At last Uncle Bub came up and we got some sticks and poked him out. And then O boy! Muggsy did shake hin. I tried to skin but it did not work very good.

        Charles

22 th day   July 1, 1944

Muggsy and I went wood chuck hunting. Uncle Henry and Mildred Frances and her friend came over to see us.

        Charles

23 th day   July 2, 1944

Timmy Glaeys and Harold came up to see us. I went to Sunday School today.

        Charles

24 th day   July 3, 1944

I have been talking to mama daddy Johny and Trixy on the telephone. I went fishing with Dicky Thomas. He caught three suckers and a red - fin salmon, I caught two suckers thats all. A man said "hay you get out of there."

        Charles

25 th day   July 4, 1944

The Fourth of July our nations birthday. We cerebrated the Fourth by haveing a picnic. I had a few caps left over from last year.

        Charles

26 th day   July 5, 1944

I went swimming with grammy. We had a of fun. Today is Uncle Sherwin's birthday he is 31 years old. I drove the horses for Uncle Sherwin.

Charles

27 th day   July 6, 1944

I finished reading the second Roy Blakely book and started reading Injun and Whitey.

Charles

28 th day   July 7, 1944

Uncle bub came up today. I went down simming with Grandma today.

Charles

29 th day   July 8, 1944

I drove the hay truck for Uncle Milo today. We finished the meadow east of the road.

Charles

30 th day   July 9, 1944

I went to Sunday school today. I took my lunch up on the big rock and ate it. I cut my knee on a nail, and spilled paper dye down my back. Joan fell through some rotten boards and landed on some sawdust.

Charles

31 th day   July 10, 1944

Uncle Sherwin bought me a new cow boy straw hat. I like it a lot. Today was the "miserablest" hay-day we had so far. They vaccinated the little pigs today

Charles

32 <u>th</u> day   July 11, 1944

I had a card from mommy and she said thet we had eight babiey rabbits. Robert Muggsy and I got a wood chuck today and we skinned him.

Charles

33 <u>th</u> day   July 12, 1944

Muggsy and I caught an other woodchuck today and skinned her. Robert came up again today. We had another thunder shower today.

Charles

34 <u>th</u> day   July 13, 1944

Muggsy cornered a woodchuck in a rock in Uncle Henrys pasture, but we could not get him out. Nothing much happened today.

Charles

35 <u>th</u> day   July 14, 1944

At last one job for the year. I got my Jack and Jill and three weekly readere today. We drew in ten loads of hay today.

Charles

36 <u>th</u> day   July 15, 1944

Daddy Monny Johnny and Trixy. I went to the warehouse with Daddy. Daddy got me five boxes of Winchester air rifle shot. I have started to feed the hens today.

Charles

37 th day   July 16, 1944

I went to Sunday school today. We went over to Uncle Clarences folks and saw his baby colt. We saw Uncle Guis folks to. Daddy mamma Johnny and Trixy went home today

      Charles

38 th day   July 17, 1944

I started going to daily vacation Bible school today. I rode down with Mr. Hack and Mrs. Hack came after us. They were 24 in my glaaa. Dicky came over and we went fishing. Jane Thomas nearly drowned the other day.

      Charles

39 th day   July 18, 1944

the mechanic came up and fixed the hay truck. I received a card from momma. She said one of the little bunnies white died.

      Charles

40 th day   July 19, 1944

they got the hay tuck fixed. Dicky came over to go fishing with me and afterwardes we played cowboys and rustlere. I helped Grandma and aunt Ellrena pick peas but I ate more then I picked. I shucked them for Grandma

      Charles

41 th day   July 20, 1944

I went down street with aunt Ellrena Gandma Uncle Sherwin and Larry. I had ten cents to spend but I could not find any thing thet was worth it so I did not spend it.

      Charles

42 <u>th</u> day   July 21, 1944

Dicky and the Russell boys came to play with me. We went fishing and no luck as usual. Uncle Sherwin put up a swing and we played croqet.

Charles

42 <u>th</u> day   July 22, 1944

The men started puting hay in the horse barn and I called off for the men. Harold Gladys Timmy and Aunt Etta came up today.

Charles

43 <u>th</u> day   July 23, 1944

I went to Sunday school today. Muggsy and I caught a woodchuck in the big rock and I set a trap for one. I went in simming and cut my big toe

Charles

44 <u>th</u> day   July 24, 1944

I started as private and turned from private to corporal and from corporal to sergeant. We had a thuner shower today. The men got in eight loads of hay today

Charles

45 <u>th</u> day   July 25, 1944

I made a hunting knife out of an old butcher knife. Geneva had a nose bleed today. I went out hunting with my bow and arrows.

Charles

46 th day   July 26, 1944

I cut some sticks to make some arrows. I called off for the men
west of the big barn and the sun was hot

Charles

47 th day

today Is my

birthday   July 27, 1944

Mommy and Daddy sent me a hack saw soft ball candy and a
book. I got two books two dollars and two packages of gum. I
had a birthday cake and a little party. Joan came down and played
with me.

Charles

48 th day   July 28, 1944

Daily vacation Bille school ended today. For learning Bible verses
they gave prizes. I received a prize, it was a black walnut letter opener.

Charles

49 th day   July 29, 1944

We had a thunder showee but we were lucky for we only had a
small load out. I tried to find a bow stick but I have not found
one yet.

Charles

50 th day   July 30, 1944

I went to sunday school today. Uncle Milo made me a case for
my knife out of a piece of rubber hose. We had a thunder shower
today

Charles

51 <u>th</u> day   July 31, 1944

I took up my woodchuck trap today. I had no luck in traping. I tied up my woodchuck pelt. I made a tomy hawk today.

Charles

52 <u>th</u> day   August 1, 1944

the men drew in twelve loads of hay today. Today has been a very good hay day. Joe Thomas (dog) and Muggsy had a bloody battle today. they nsever seem to be friendly. Billy drove Silver down here.

Charles

51 <u>th</u> day   August 2, 1944

we had a thunder shower today. the men got up all the hay before the shower. the men filled up the horse barn today

Charles

52 <u>th</u> day   August 3, 1944

Perley killed a snake and I killed one. I skinned one. I lost my supper and my knife today. We finished haying today.

Charles

53 <u>th</u> day   August 4, 1944

We had a 4H meeting today. We went to Chittenden after a cow. She was going to have a calf but she had all ready had her calf. We did not get there soon enough.

Charles

53 <u>th</u> day   August 5, 1944

Billy came down and let me ride his poney. We had some watermelon today. The men put up the hay machines.

Charles

54 <u>th</u> day   August 6, 1944

I went to Sunday School today. Uncle Milo and I walked down by the river today. We had pop corn tonight.

Charles

55 <u>th</u> day   August 7, 1944

The men built a fence around the meadow and I help them. We had blackberrie short cake and corn today.

Charles

56 <u>th</u> day   August 8, 1944

I went to Chittenden today   I helped get the miserable old cattle back in where they belong. We fixed the fence up in Chittenden. I went over to Center Rutland with Grandma and Uncle Milo.

Charles

57 <u>th</u> day   August 9, 1944

The men went up and fixed the fence and mowed thistles. I saw a woochuck today.

Charles

58 <u>th</u> day   August 10, 1944

I walked home from Chittenden about nine miles. We drove down two steers and three cwos. Grandma Fish sent me the book Lasssie come home.

Charles

59 <u>th</u> day   August 11, 1944

Barbara came up last night. There is a 4H meeting tonight. Uncle Milo sold my papers and my magazines today. I got $1.65 for them.

Charles

60 <u>th</u> day   August 12, 1944

Daddy John trixie and mama came down today. I went to a farm bureau picnic, and went simiming in lake Bomoseen.

Charles

61 <u>th</u> day   August 13, 1944

I went to sunday school today. I went swimming in the old swimming pool today. I played with Daddy and John tonight.

Charles

62 <u>th</u> day   August 14, 1944

I went to the dentist and had four six year old molars filled. I saw Grandma Fish today.

Charles

63 days   August 15, 1944

Barby and I rode down after the garbage on the back of the truck. We went swimming today.

Charles

64 days   August 16, 1944

I went swimming in Davis swimming hole and down under bridge. We all went up to have supper with aunt Ellrena

Charles

65 days   August 15, 1944

I went over to Uncle Guys today.

Charles

66 days   August 15, 1944

I went swimming with daddy today

Charles

66 days   August 16, 1944

I went to Rutland today. Mama brought me some comist. Daddy cut brush for Uncle Guy.

Charles

67 days   August 17, 1944

I went on a pisnic today, on the shore of lake St. Catherine.

Charles

67 days   August 18, 1944

We are over to Uncle Clarences' today.

Charles

68 days   August 18, 1944

I hunted red squirrels today.

Charles

69 days   August 19, 1944

I went to Bible school today.

Charles

70 days   August 20, 1944

We came back to Gandmas today.

71 days   August 21, 1944

I went up in the atti and got down some old books. I am going to sell them.

Charles

72 days   August 22, 1944

I went to Chittenden today. Mama bought me a Indian hat.

Charles